To Nadine
on your birthday (23)

Every blessing today
& always.

With much love

Mum & Dad.

xxx
xx
x

(December 2012)

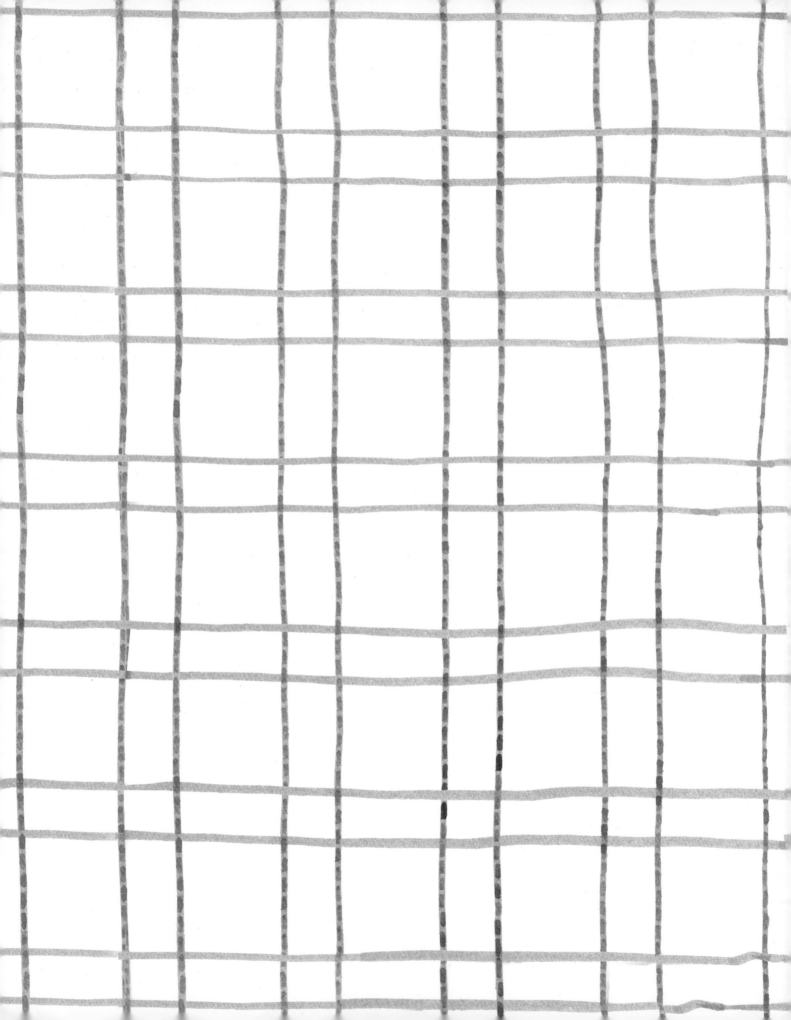

FRESH & EASY

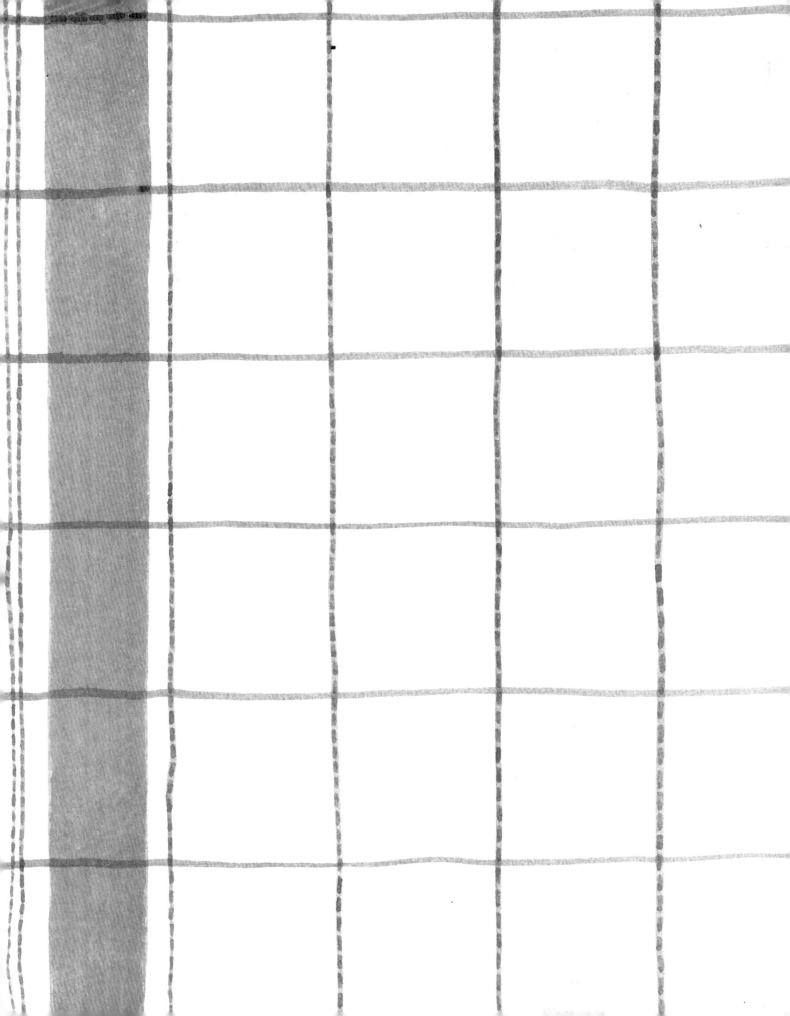

What to Cook & How to Cook it:
FRESH & EASY

JANE HORNBY

As winter turns to spring and nature comes to life, so do our taste buds. Gone are the cravings for hearty pies and desserts—we want lighter cooking, fresher food that won't keep us cooped up indoors for too long. But despite the longer evenings, warmer days and explosion of ingredients in the aisles, there's still that same dilemma that faces us all: what to cook?

Fresh & Easy is a collection of spring and summer classics, plus some of the ways I like to cook with seasonal ingredients—ideal for when you want to cook something lighter, fresher or just more unusual. Each dish uses one or more of the season's best products (be it fruit, vegetables or herbs), will look and taste impressive, and won't stress you out in the making.

To me, "fresh" translates into recipes that are bright, intense and vibrant, with each dish staying true to its core ingredients and letting them shine through. Good-quality fresh fruit and vegetables are so delicious, they often need little or no cooking, and less preparation: the simpler the better.

I hope to show you how to create easy meals and provide inspiration when yours runs dry. How about the perfect seafood risotto? Or maybe a refreshing fruit salad with lime and coconut instead of cereal in the morning? There's something for every occasion, with chapters defined by the kind of meal you want to serve rather than by food type, from Breakfast & Brunch and Quick Lunches & Suppers to Barbecues and Desserts. Plus, I've suggested menu combinations to make entertaining easy. Many of the recipes can be scaled up or down too, depending on how many people you're feeding. All you need to do is read through the recipes, shop and cook.

What can you expect to find as you flick through the pages? Punchy and refreshing tastes of the Mediterranean, Middle East, Asia and even Scandinavia, plus popular family outdoor cooking. The picnic recipes are easily transported and won't go soggy, and most of the grilling (barbecue) recipes can be cooked ahead of time to make things easy as well as keeping food safe (more of this later on in Eating Outdoors on page 11).

You'll find that many of the recipes are flexible. Some of the brunches make a great quick supper, some sides make terrific lunchbox fillers, and some picnic food will also make an excellent appetizer or lunch. Many of the recipes come with their own sides built in, which can also be treated as individual recipes if you like.

If you're a beginner cook or someone who feels alienated rather than inspired by other more "cheffy" books, then let's start your cooking journey here, together. Believe me, anyone can cook from this book. Just read through the sections that follow this introduction before you dive in, as there's plenty of helpful information that will set you on the course for success. More experienced cooks will find new ideas, tips, and twists, or perhaps the ultimate recipe when others have failed. These recipes have been written with your cooking dilemmas in mind, with potential questions and queries answered along the way. I've set out to create a really useful book, written with down-to-earth practicality that eliminates the guesswork.

Why step by step? From my experience as a food writer, I know how valuable it is to have a guiding hand through new recipes and techniques. All the recipes are accompanied by step-by-step instructions and super-clear photographs to ensure that when you follow the recipe, you're seeing what I did and will know that you're on the right track. Also, the ingredients have been photographed clearly to help with the shopping—I find this also helps to jog the memory for what's already in the pantry (storecupboard), fridge or freezer.

The recipes are written to make the most of the time and ingredients you have. That's why all the chopping instructions are in the recipe, rather than the ingredients list, so that you don't waste time prepping when there will be time to fill later on. I've added make-ahead tips wherever relevant because just like you, I don't find it fun sweating over lots of last-minute cooking and often need to fit it around my workload during the week.

I won't assume that you know complicated cooking terminology or that you have endless space, time, or budget to create your next meal. Neither will I call for any bizarre or expensive equipment (everything you need is listed on page 14). I've added lots of little tricks and tips along the way to help you to understand what's going on, and even, in some cases, what to do if something goes wrong.

Cooking fresh is about thinking fresh, too, and one of the things I love most is helping cooks to break out of their norm and try something new. It may sound crazy, but I love to watch people shop and confess to collecting left-behind shopping lists from baskets and shopping carts (trolleys). And it's amazing how little they change throughout the year. Picture yourself wandering around the supermarket. What do you pick up? Is it the same few items week after week? Why not

shake things up and try some of the wonderful produce that's available? A good way to start is to think of fresh produce as the hero for more of your meals. Try building a dish around seasonal ingredients, then adding simply-cooked meat, fish or eggs to the mix to make a fresh meal that's balanced toward healthy eating. Even my meatier recipes have a fresh element, be it an accompanying side, dip or salad.

I'll introduce you to a few unusual ingredients along the way, but will always give an alternative. I try not to use half pots of ingredients either, so that there's nothing left hanging around in the fridge. Owners of *What to Cook and How to Cook It* will already know how much I love my pantry. Having a well-stocked pantry and freezer makes it possible to pop to the store for just the few fresh ingredients you need and will save you money in the long run (there's more about this on page 17). If you're keen on gardening, then the recipes in this book are ideal for using up produce from the garden or allotment too.

Of course, the seasons and what's available in stores and markets will vary from region to region, but regardless of where you live, try and buy locally produced food, shop in season as much as you can, and spend as much as your wallet allows. Why? Because, wherever you live, you'll reap the rewards in your cooking. Food that gets to you faster will be fresher, tastier and needs less doing to it to make it taste good. Cooking "fresh" makes your life easier. And what could be better than that?

Jane Hornby

How to Make the Recipes Work for You

1

Read the recipe from start to finish before you start cooking. This will familiarize you with what's about to happen, and what to look for.

2

Unless you're a confident cook, don't change the ingredients in a recipe. You can always make it again once you're familiar with the basics. If you do have to make substitutions, try to swap like for like: use white sugar for brown sugar, not honey or sweetener. Baking recipes, in particular, have a careful balance of ingredients that shouldn't be scaled up or down.

3

Weigh and measure everything carefully, especially when baking. All spoons are level, unless stated otherwise. American cup and ounce measures, or European metric measures have been used throughout, but stick to one system only for good results. Australian tablespoons are 20 ml, so Australian readers should use 3 teaspoons in place of 1 tablespoon.

4

The preparation time at the start of the recipe indicates the amount of time you will spend weighing and chopping ingredients, and includes any preliminary cooking, such as preparing a sauce or browning meat. The cooking time refers to the final stage of cooking. In some cases you'll be near the stove the whole time, such as when making a quick soup. In recipes with longer cooking times, this is when you can go and do something else. Ovens and stoves will vary. Use your nose, eyes and ears to tell you what's going on, and set a timer. Ask yourself, is it golden? Does it smell good? Is it bubbling in the middle?

5

Always preheat the oven and keep the door closed; peeking every few minutes will lower the oven temperature. I advise you to use an oven thermometer to check that your oven is correctly calibrated. If grilling (barbecuing), see the tips on page 12.

6

Take note of the instructions alongside each ingredient. Softened butter should be very soft, almost like mayonnaise. Meat should be allowed to come up to room temperature before it is cooked or your cooking times won't tally with mine. Eggs should also be at room temperature for baking.

7

Taste as you go. Good cooks constantly taste their food; it's the only way you'll know if the sauce is seasoned enough, reduced enough or spicy enough.

8

Warm your plates in the oven when serving hot food, especially something with sauce or gravy.

9

Frozen desserts are usually best frozen overnight and then given 20 minutes or so in the fridge before serving. If it's a hot day, put your serving plate in the freezer for a few minutes.

10

Keep cold things cold for as long as possible to keep them in prime condition. Always dress salads at the last minute, unless the recipe states otherwise.

11

Unless otherwise specified, all herbs are fresh; all pepper is freshly ground black pepper; all salt is good-quality kosher or flaky sea salt; eggs are extra large (UK large), all vegetables are medium-size and milk is reduced fat (semi-skimmed). Where possible, use unrefined (golden), superfine (caster) sugar for baking.

Eating Outdoors

Picnics and barbecues are great fun, but can be a bit daunting if you're the cook, so preparation is key. Follow the steps below, ask for as much help as possible and you'll be fine. All the picnic and grilling (barbecue) recipes are ideal for enjoying indoors too. There's an "if it rains" back-up plan so there's no need to cancel or stand outdoors with a golf umbrella.

Food hygiene

First, let's talk about food hygiene. Not a nice subject, but one of real importance when cooking for a picnic or barbecue. Bacteria love lukewarm temperatures, so food left out in the sun or even at room temperature all day makes the perfect breeding ground for bugs that can cause stomach upsets. Always follow these basic rules to be food safe:

• Always wash your hands thoroughly with soap and water before you start cooking and after handling raw meat, fish, or poultry.

• Keep food in the fridge for as long as possible before you take it outside.

• Always use separate knives, boards, and utensils for cooked and raw food, and keep raw and cooked food separate.

• Keep food covered so that insects or animals don't dine with you.

• If you're not serving it immediately, cool food as quickly as you can once it has been cooked, even if you are going to reheat it. When reheating, make sure it is piping hot to the middle. This is important for pasta, rice, and other grains as well as meat and fish. A fast way to cool food down is to spread it out in a thin layer over a large surface. Don't put hot food into the fridge as it will increase the temperature of the food already in there.

• Keep raw meat and fish at the bottom of the fridge so it can't drip onto food that's ready to eat.

Picnics

There's no need for a fancy wicker hamper—anyone can head out for a picnic with a few bits of basic equipment.

• Pack food into an insulated bag or box and use plenty of ice packs to keep food chilled. Another useful way to keep food cool is to freeze any plastic bottles or cartons of drinks and tuck them around the food. They will thaw on the way to the picnic and keep everything cool.

• Paper plates and cups will be cheap and easy to carry, but won't do for a smart picnic. Don't take glass—it's too dangerous—pick up some sturdy plastic ones instead.

• A large flask is ideal for hot or cold drinks or soup. Give it a really good wash before filling.

• Take a serrated knife, a small chopping board and don't forget the knives and forks and something to serve with.

• Don't try and make too many things— see page 341 for a few simple picnic menu ideas. You can always ask friends to bring a dish with them too.

• For safety, avoid taking risky items. In general, it's best to avoid shellfish or recipes using raw or lightly cooked eggs, meat, or fish at picnics.

• Keep dressings separate so that salad greens (leaves) don't get soggy.

• Take cakes or tarts along in the pan they were made in, and just wrap the top with aluminum foil.

• Take antibacterial wipes with you, and plenty of paper towels or napkins.

- And finally, be a considerate picnicker and take a bag for your garbage (rubbish).

Barbecues

It's nice to throw a spontaneous barbecue, but you should have certain key equipment on hand to make the experience more pleasurable and safer for you. You'll need:

- Long tongs or a long spatula (fish slice) for turning food without scorching your arms

- A long oven mitt (glove)

- Long metal skewers are handy if you want to serve kebabs. Wooden skewers must be soaked in cold water for 30 minutes before use, and can still char a little

- A flat table or surface on which to set aside raw and cooked food and for your seasonings, marinades, and so on

- A heatproof brush for basting meat as it cooks

- A water spray bottle to damp down any flames that come from drips of fat or marinade

- A large bowl of warm water with soap and clean paper towels for hand washing

There's a huge range of grills (barbecues) out there, from basic kettles with charcoal to monster grills with several gas burners, thermostatic controls, and so on. I don't even have a backyard so developed all of the grilling (barbecue) recipes at my friends' and family's homes, which proves that they can be cooked just about anywhere, on anything!

For the sake of some kind of brevity, I'm going to assume that you have an average-size charcoal grill that has one rack and a lid, and that you're not a seasoned pro. For your first attempt, choose one or two recipes to be cooked on the grill, and add a couple of easy salads or sides.

To make life easier, I prefer to partially cook dishes as much as I can ahead of time in the oven: let's use chicken legs as an example. The legs are roasted in the oven until fully cooked through but not quite tender. I can then put them straight onto the grill until tender and crisp, or chill and finish them off later on or the next day. It may not be authentic, but I'm all about making life easy, plus it takes away any anxiety about whether meat is fully cooked. This is the way I cook ribs and even sausages, too. Smaller, quick-cooking items such as burgers and shrimp (prawns) can be cooked directly on the grill. There are relevant instructions in each recipe.

A charcoal grill should be lit about 30 minutes before you want to start cooking, and needs to be burning without smoke or flames leaping up. The coals will be white or gray rather than black, glowing underneath and giving off a nice, even heat. The equivalent temperature for a gas or thermo-controlled grill is 400°F (200°C).

Before you begin cooking, check that the bars of the grill are clean. Old food residues will not only affect the taste of your food, but will also increase the chances of it sticking. Use a grill brush or rub a scrunched-up piece of aluminum foil up and down the bars with your tongs to loosen any bits.

For the best heat control, create hotter and cooler areas. To do this, mound the coals up toward one side of the grill, then shelve them down to the other side. The hottest part, where the coals are deepest, will be ideal for quick, direct cooking.

Transfer bigger pieces of meat to the cooler side to finish cooking indirectly with the lid on. If you have a gas grill, then leaving one side of the grill off will have the same effect.

Use the lid as much as you can, as it will make cooking more efficient. Just remember to keep checking under there.

Unless you're very experienced, avoid cooking very large pieces of meat on a charcoal grill, as it's likely that the coals will need to be replenished throughout the cooking time.

Meat will cook more evenly if it isn't cold. Remove from the fridge around 30 minutes before you want to cook, keep it covered and out of the sun.

Avoid turning food too quickly or too often. When the food is ready, it will lift away easily. If something really has stuck and you're concerned that it's overcooking, then ease it away with a spatula (fish slice) rather than pulling it off with your tongs. If you like, you can sit an ovenproof pan on the grill and treat it like a giant stove. This is handy for cooking fish, or if you're afraid of losing small bits of food down between the grates.

To cook fish the traditional way, first oil the grill with a heatproof brush to prevent the skin from sticking.

Sweet or oily marinades will easily blister and burn and cause flare-ups, so wipe excess marinade away before cooking. And do not baste cooked food with marinade that's been in contact with uncooked food.

Make your salads and sides ahead of time, then finish them off at the last minute.

And finally, rope in a trusted helper— someone on stand-by to take away used plates, deliver the food to your guests and pass you a beer now and again. Then sit down, join in, and relax.

Here's what you'll need to make all the recipes in this book, aside from anything special for barbecues or picnics (see pages 11–12). All the basics are available in most houseware and kitchen stores, so there's no need to spend a lot of money on special equipment.

Chopping boards

You'll need two boards: one for raw food and one for cooked. Plastic boards are hard-wearing and easier to clean. If you prefer wooden boards, choose a good-quality wood. Don't leave it soaking in water or the wood may split. Wooden boards hold smells more readily, so I keep one side for smelly food and one for non-smelly. To stop it from slipping, dampen some paper towel and put it under the board.

Knives

You'll only need a few knives for the recipes here. Firstly, a chef's knife with a blade of about 8 inches (20 cm), but this will depend on your own hand size— ask in a cookshop for advice. Choose one that feels comfortable in your hand, not too light or heavy, and that can be rocked on its blade to allow you to chop in one swift movement. Next, a knife with a blade about 4 inches (10 cm) long is useful for smaller jobs. A small serrated knife will be handy when preparing soft fruit. Finally, a bread knife and a frosting spatula (palette knife), which is good for getting underneath cookies and other delicate things without damaging them. Blunt knives are dangerous because they're more likely to slip, so keep knives sharp using a steel or a sharpening tool. If you are cooking these recipes with children, ensure that they are supervised at all times when using knives. A small, serrated knife with an easy-to-grip plastic handle is the safest option here.

Mixing bowls

One large, one medium and a couple of small bowls for mixing should be enough. Pyrex bowls are good because they can withstand heat and their depth prevents splashes.

Serving bowls & dishes

You can use your largest mixing bowl for serving, although it's likely to be in service doing something else if you're cooking more than one thing. Perhaps something plastic or bamboo and light-weight would be best (and unbreakable) if you are heading out into the garden to eat. I find a large white platter makes anything look good, plus a nice cake plate or stand with a flat bottom is perfect for serving cakes and tarts. A set of small sundae glasses or bowls is ideal for serving dessert, but tumblers or coffee cups are just as good.

Measuring pitchers (jugs)

2½-cup (600-ml) and 1-quart (1-litre) measuring pitchers are useful, ideally made of heatproof glass or plastic. If you have to choose just one, a smaller pitcher is more useful for measuring small quantities, and you can always refill it.

Pans

You'll need small, medium and large pans. The large one should be deep enough for boiling plenty of water for pasta or potatoes. You'll also need a large skillet or frying pan, ideally about 9½ inches (24 cm) across for most of your frying, and a smaller one of about 8 inches (20 cm) is also handy for frittatas and omelets. A grill pan (griddle) is ideal if you like the char-grilled look. If you're new to cooking, go for nonstick pans, but remember that quality really counts, as you're going to be using them every day. Look for pans with a thick base, which will conduct heat evenly. Choose pans with heatproof handles and lids so that you can put them under the broiler (grill) or in the oven. Glass lids are great, as you can see what's happening inside without losing heat.

Stove-to-oven pan

Although I've used it far less in this book than the last, I'd still recommend that the most useful pan of all is a large, shallow one that can go on the stove and into the oven. It will double as a skillet (frying pan) and roasting pan and can be put under the broiler (grill) too. Make sure the handles are ovenproof. A nonstick interior is helpful but not essential. Take extra care with cast-iron pans on the stove, as the metal conducts heat very quickly and stays hot for a long time.

Roasting pans

Choose the sturdiest roasting pans you can find, as thin pans can warp when used directly on the stove or in the oven at high temperatures. You'll need a large one with fairly tall sides. A small one is also useful for smaller pieces of meat, as the juices will evaporate less.

Baking sheets & pans

A large baking sheet with a lip of about 1¼ inches (3 cm) is useful, as is one with a lip along one edge only. For these recipes I have also used a standard 1-quart (1-litre) loaf pan measuring about 8 × 4 inches (20 × 11 cm) across the top; a fluted 9-inch (23-cm) tart pan; a 12-hole muffin pan; an 8 × 12-inch (20 × 30-cm) brownie pan; two shallow 8-inch (20-cm) loose-bottom cake pans, a deep 8-inch (20-cm) round cake pan and a 9-inch (23-cm) round springform pan.

Baking dishes

A couple of good-quality, ceramic baking dishes (also known sometimes as oven-to-tableware) will come in useful for cooking and serving. Go for dishes with handles, if you can. A large one would be about 12 inches (30 cm) long and 8 inches (20 cm) across. Small ovenproof dishes about 6 inches (15 cm) across, are ideal for the baked eggs on page 32 or for making individual portions for the freezer.

Weighing scales

In the UK, weighing scales are essential for baking. If you want to buy some, look for ones that measure in at least 5-g (⅛ oz) or smaller increments and which can be easily wiped clean.

Measuring cups & spoons

Metal or plastic cups and spoons are fine. I always take mine off the ring they come on to avoid washing the whole set when I've only used one. Some spoons are too large to fit into the necks of small jars, so a set of narrow spoons can be useful.

Hand-held blender

Easy to use, quick to clean and small to store, a hand-held stick or immersion blender makes a great addition to the kitchen as it can be used to puree and blend almost anything. Most come with a tall pitcher (jug) and some have a mini-chopper attachment too, which is ideal for grinding spices or chopping herbs.

Food processor

A food processor will save a lot of time, as it can chop, grind and mix much more quickly than even the fastest cook. It is particularly good for making pastry, as the blades keep dough cool and won't overwork the flour, guaranteeing you a tender crust. Choose a straightforward processor with a good-sized bowl. Don't worry about buying one with lots of attachments; you'll hardly ever use them.

Hand-held electric mixer

This is a must-have for baking. It adds air and lightness to cake batters, whips cream quickly and can beat out lumps. You may prefer to use a stand mixer instead, although these are much more expensive.

Other useful equipment

• a box grater with coarse and fine sides (or invest in a microplane grater, which is ideal for grating citrus fruit zest and whole nutmeg)
• a pastry brush
• a rolling pin
• a lemon juicer
• a ladle
• some wooden spoons (long handles are best)
• a rubber spatula
• a pair of tongs for serving pasta and turning food
• a vegetable peeler
• pie weights (baking beans)
• a wire cooling rack
• a balloon whisk
• a strainer (sieve)
• a colander
• an ice-cream scoop
• a spatula (fish slice) for turning delicate food and lifting onto serving plates
• some parchment paper (the nonstick kind, which is different from ordinary waxed greaseproof paper), plastic wrap (clingfilm) and a roll of aluminum foil
• sealable plastic food storage bags

Ovens

Familiarize yourself with your oven. Does it have conventional heat, in other words a heating element at the top and bottom of the oven, or is it a convection (fan-assisted) oven?

Conventional electric ovens

These are hotter at the top and bottom, closer to the elements, so it's best to bake cakes and roast large cuts of meat in the middle to make sure you don't burn the tops. Put things that you want to brown or crisp up a little more, such as roasted potatoes, in the top third.

Convection (fan-assisted) ovens

The oven temperatures in this book are for conventional ovens. In most cases, you should set the temperature of a convection oven 68°F (20°C) lower than that of a conventional oven, but the cooking time will stay the same. This is because convection ovens cook food more quickly, as the hot air circulates around the food. However, do check your oven's instructions, as models vary and some temperature displays do the adjustment automatically for you. The heat from a convection oven is even, so it doesn't matter where you put the food. Convection ovens tend to need less time to preheat.

Gas ovens

These have roughly three zones of heat, the bottom being the coolest and the top the hottest. Cook anything that needs to be browned in the top third of the oven, cakes and roasts in the middle, and anything that needs gentle cooking at the bottom.

Your fridge & freezer

Hotter weather makes it harder work for fridges and freezers to keep cold. Overcrowding your fridge will prevent the cool air from circulating, creating warm pockets of air, which will encourage bacteria to grow. Meat, fish, dairy and other highly perishable food should be kept in the coldest part of the fridge, which is normally the bottom, but not in the vegetable drawer. The manual will tell you more. Aim to keep the coldest part of the fridge between 32°F and 41°F (0°C and 5°C) and keep a fridge thermometer in there to check the temperature regularly. If you know you're going to be short on space when entertaining, keep drinks cool in large buckets of ice instead of the fridge, as the food should take priority.

Conversely, freezers function best when they're full. The optimum temperature is 0.4°F (-18°C). Defrost the freezer regularly if it doesn't do it automatically. Put newly-purchased chilled or frozen food into the fridge or freezer as soon as you can, don't put hot food into the fridge to cool, and don't refreeze thawed food (see page 19–20).

Buying & Storing Fresh Ingredients

The first step to successful cooking is to start with really good-quality ingredients. Here's where I'll take you through what to look for in the store and the market. The focus is mainly on fruit and vegetables, but I'll touch on meat, fish, and dairy products too.

All the ingredients in this book are available from major supermarkets, but it's a good idea to try your local markets and retailers, as they often sell produce more cheaply and have more connections with local growers and producers. Your local butcher and fish, fruit and vegetable suppliers are there to help too, so don't be daunted. If you're new to cooking, they will be only too pleased to tell you more about what's available, and the more regularly you go, the more likely they are to throw in the odd perk for being a loyal customer! Spend whatever you can afford on fish, meat and eggs—you'll notice the difference.

Fruit & vegetables
We've all done it—bought lots of fruit and vegetables and thrown it away a week later. Shopping carefully and storing properly should stop this from happening. Don't be swayed by "buy one get one free" offers unless you really are going to eat everything within a week and have enough storage space to keep it in tip-top condition.

Shopping at the farmers' market allows you to shop "greener," reducing the number of food miles the food has travelled. If you're not familiar with what is seasonal, then a market is the best place to find out. If it's labelled as "local" and there's lots of it, then it's in season. Often there's a chance to try interesting heirloom or heritage varieties that you just won't find in the supermarket because they aren't grown in the quantities that the big chains

demand. If you're shopping in the supermarket, study the labels to see where something has come from. They don't make it easy for us: for example, as I write, it's the peak of the bean season in the UK, yet at my local store there are green beans grown 30 miles away from London (where I live, and so relatively "local"), sitting alongside beans from Kenya. Check labels and ask for help, and if you can't find what you need, don't be afraid to make substitutions.

When shopping for fruit and vegetables always choose those that feel heavy for their size. Don't worry too much about looking for perfection (misshapen ones are often the tastiest) and you'll find it hard to find regulation-length cucumbers at any farmers' market or farm shop in any case. Avoid anything mushy, with obvious soft patches, holes or rotten bits, and take it out of the wrapping before storing.

Wash all fruit and vegetables well before using them, too, since even if they look clean they can contain small bits of grit or agricultural residues. Trim away any tough outer leaves and peel root vegetables if you like. Many vitamins and nutrients lie just beneath the skin, so don't peel down too far (or leave the skins on and scrub them with a good stiff brush if you'd prefer).

"Fruiting" vegetables, such as bell peppers, eggplants (aubergines), zucchini (courgettes), cucumbers, tomatoes, avocados and squash, should be firm and plump without dark patches or squishy spots. Raw bell peppers, eggplants and squash don't need to be chilled. Choose slimmer zucchini and cucumbers, as they tend to be less watery and have fewer seeds, and keep these in the fridge.

Let avocados ripen at room temperature (the skin will turn darker and the flesh will yield slightly at the top), then chill until needed. Tomatoes are best left at room temperature unless they are really ripe and you can't use them up, as chilling deadens the taste. Melons might seem out of place here, but they are from the same family as squash and cucumbers. So a ripe melon should give slightly when pressed at the stalk end, and have a distinct musky melon smell. Once ripe, store melons in the fridge, but let them come up to room temperature before eating.

Stalks, bulbs and stems such as celery, fennel, leeks, and scallions (spring onions) should not be limp or yellowed, but fresh, pale green, and white (unless you're using red varieties). Keep them chilled if you can. Regular onions can be stored in a cool dark place. Rhubarb (which is a vegetable used as a fruit) should be firm, and thinner stems will be less stringy and quicker to cook. Asparagus needs to be sparklingly fresh or it can taste bitter and old. The tips should be wrinkle-free, bright, and firm, and they should snap when bent.

Salad greens (leaves) and lettuce are best washed, dried, and then stored in a plastic bag in the drawer at the bottom of the fridge. When buying, avoid heads with brown or dull patches or that look limp. Often with larger lettuces, you'll need to strip away the first few leaves as they can be a little tough. Bagged salads can be convenient, but can turn soggy very quickly and are often much more expensive than buying whole heads or handfuls of greens (leaves).

Green leafy vegetables and brassicas, such as spinach, cabbages and broccoli, should be firm and again have no sign of discoloring. Hard white, red and Chinese cabbages are wonderful for slaws. Their leaves should be tightly packed. I prefer to use salad or baby spinach, as it doesn't need much preparation aside from washing, but if you can only find the big stuff, trim off any thick stalks and veins first. Broccoli should be bushy and intensely green or with a slightly purple hue.

Herbs of all kinds should be perky and bright, without any sign of yellowing. To extend the life of cut herbs, wrap the bunch in a sheet of wet paper towel, then seal into a food storage bag or plastic container and chill. If you change the paper every few days, the herbs will still be super-fresh after a week. Harder herbs like thyme and rosemary will last longer than softer herbs like basil and cilantro (coriander). Store sprouts like alfalfa the same way, taking care to wash them very well before use, and don't exceed the use by date.

Berries and currants are best bought on the day you want to use them, especially raspberries. If you're intending to eat them uncooked, then take out of the fridge an hour or so before eating. If you find yourself with lots of berries going off fast, then pop them in the freezer to use later for baking or desserts. Rinse fresh berries very carefully in a bowl of cold water before letting them dry on paper towels. A way to tell if berries, currants, or grapes are fresh is to look at the tops and stems—the greener they are, the fresher they'll be.

Stone fruits such as peaches, apricots, and plums are often sold either very under-ripe ("for home ripening") or ripe and ready. Home-ripening fruit (which tends to mean hard as bullets) should be unwrapped and ripened in a fruit bowl out of direct sunlight, which may take a few days. When ripe, chill until needed. Cherries are best chilled and eaten within a day or two. Rather than over-ripening and becoming mushy, they seem to lose their intensity. Again, enjoy stone fruit at room temperature.

Potatoes and root vegetables may be a winter mainstay, but spring and summer is a great time to experiment with the babies: young beets (beetroot), carrots, new potatoes, and radishes are all ideal for salads and sides. Keep in the fridge if there's room. Leave the skins on new potatoes, as they taste better when cooked in their skins. Avoid green potatoes, and any root vegetables that are limp, wrinkled or sprouting. Main-crop potatoes and carrots and some other root vegetables are also still available, as farmers keep them in cold storage ready to sell throughout the year.

Pods and husks such as green beans, peas, fava (broad) beans, runner beans and sweet corn are wonderful when fresh, but can deteriorate fast. Smaller bean pods tend to be the sweetest and most tender, especially in the case of fava beans, and all green beans should snap sharply when bent. Keep in the fridge until you need them. If an ear (cob) of corn still has its green husk on, peel back one of the leaves and check that the kernels are plump and yellow. The fresher the corn, the sweeter it will be. Frozen peas and beans are very useful time-savers and can often be fresher than the "fresh" stuff on the shelves, as they are frozen soon after picking. I like to use frozen fava beans when fresh ones are out of season, or if I'm feeling too lazy to pod them myself. Also, I prefer frozen peas to eat, and sometimes use frozen soy beans instead of either peas or beans.

Exotic fruits all have their own little foibles. A ripe mango will yield ever so slightly to your thumb at the stem end, and should smell fragrant. A decent pineapple will smell fruity. If you pull a leaf from the center of the crown and it comes away easily, the pineapple is ripe. Passion fruit buck the trend: wrinkly is good. Pomegranates should be blushing from bright pink to purple, and figs will be plump and heavy and smell fragrant. Bananas are best when the skin is a uniform yellow. To speed up the ripening of bananas (and avocados), put them into a paper bag with an apple or two. Apples release ethylene, a gas which kick-starts the ripening process. Keep all tropical fruit, apart from bananas, in the fridge once ripe.

Citrus fruits—limes, lemons, oranges, and grapefruit—should feel heavy for their weight. It doesn't matter if their skin is a little blemished. Choose organic (unwaxed) if you need to use the zest as well as the juice or flesh, and keep in a cool dry place. Citrus fruit are easier to squeeze at room temperature. I sometimes even pop mine in the microwave for just a few seconds to loosen up the insides a bit. A standard lime normally gives 2 tablespoons of juice, and a standard lemon about 3 tablespoons. If yours are particularly small or large, then buy accordingly.

Apples and pears are traditionally autumnal crops, but are available throughout the year, and some early varieties will be on sale from late summer. It's funny how a rock-hard pear can suddenly ripen, and it's easy to miss the magic window between hard and mushy. Check them regularly, chill when ripe and enjoy as soon as you can. Apples will keep in a cool place for several weeks, but are best chilled for perfect crispness. Take care, as both apples and pears bruise easily.

Meat & poultry

Your butcher will trim, roll, or cut meat for you, and often give tips about how to cook it, as well as giving you the bones for making broth (stock), if you'd like to have a go. Choose meat that comes from a traceable source and has been reared to high standards of health and welfare, and free-range or organically produced meat and poultry if you can—you'll be rewarded with meat with far superior taste and texture.

Look for red meat that's well marbled with fat, is natural-looking (not gray and not an unnaturally bright red) and with a slight sheen, but not slimy. Bones should be white tinged with blueish-pink. Poultry should look as fresh as possible, without any discoloration on the skin or any bad smell. Again, choose the best you can afford.

Meat and poultry should be kept chilled for no more than 3 days and stored at the bottom of the fridge so as to avoid any drips contaminating food below. If you want to freeze meat, poultry or fish for later, wrap it well and freeze on the day of purchase. It's best to use it within a month. Frozen meat and fish should be thawed in the fridge overnight on a tray or large plate to catch any juices. Unless using frozen, try and buy fish and seafood on the day you want to cook it.

Fish

Fish suppliers will scale, fillet, and clean (gut) any fish, and should have a good range of seafood, either fresh or frozen, depending on where you live and the season. I know it can be hard to remember which fish is or isn't from endangered stocks. The best advice is to pick fish that is labelled as sustainably caught and be prepared to try a new fish at your fish supplier's recommendation. Look for bright-eyed whole fish, with shiny scales, gills that are very red inside, and no fishy smell. Look for firmness and sparkling, smooth flesh. Buying fillets can be trickier because the key indicators of freshness (the eyes and gills) have been removed. Reject anything that looks dull, feels soft, or smells overly fishy.

It's harder to detect freshness with seafood such as mussels and clams, but again use your nose as a guide; it'll soon tell you what to avoid. Sometimes frozen fish and seafood can be fresher than that labelled as fresh. This is because it is frozen at sea and has had less time to deteriorate. Shrimp (prawns) with heads on should have bright, black bulgy eyes and be without roe (eggs). Squid is best bought ready-prepared, as it's a messy job. The flesh should be pearly white and firm.

Eggs

Choose free-range eggs or organic if you can afford them; the taste is superior to that of factory-farmed eggs and the hens will have led happier lives. Eggs also need to be kept in the fridge and will last for up to three weeks. Keep them away from strong-smelling foods, as they absorb smells easily.

Dairy products

These should be stored with care. It's best to check the label, but generally milk, yogurts, soft cheeses, and cream will keep for about a week. If you're going to eat them as a separate course, most cheeses are much better served at room temperature.

Sell-by & use-by dates

The manufacturer's use-by date is the one to take notice of. The sell-by date is for the retailer and the best-before is just a guide—the food is usually fine to eat until the use-by date expires.

This book may be called *Fresh & Easy*, but that's not to say that I haven't looked to my pantry somewhere in most of the recipes. You could think of your kitchen cabinets like a wardrobe; some things come out more often than others, depending on the weather. I still believe that a well-equipped pantry is central to simple cooking. By slowly building up a collection of ingredients, you'll gradually reduce the amount of shopping you'll need to do, eventually only shopping for fresh ingredients, and the odd replacement for your pantry stock.

Oils & butter
Keep a bottle of ordinary olive oil for general cooking and one of extra-virgin olive oil for dressing and finishing a dish. Depending on where you live, cold-pressed canola (rapeseed) oil may be a more local product to choose instead of extra-virgin olive, so have a good look on the shelves. A bottle of sunflower or vegetable oil, which will have little taste and a high burning point, is a good, economical choice for sautéing or frying. Unsalted butter is best for cooking, as you can then determine the level of salt in your dish according to your taste.

Cans, jars, & tubes
Even though summer is the peak of the tomato season, I often still use canned tomatoes and pureed canned tomatoes (passata) where appropriate, plus tomato paste (purée), one of my all-time essentials. Canned legumes (pulses) such as chickpeas, canellini and black beans, are ideal for salads and salsas and can be interchanged easily. Roasted red bell peppers from a jar appear several times in this book, and they are one of my go-to ingredients when I want to add depth of flavor and ruby color. The same goes for sun-dried or sun bluched tomatoes. Ready-to-eat artichokes, olives, and other antipasti vegetables come in handy

too for salads, pastas, and pizzas. The best olives for cooking are the small, dry type, which are pitted (stoned) for convenience. Once opened, keep jars in the fridge. Make sure that the top layer is covered with liquid to keep air out.

Pasta, noodles, rice, & polenta
All of these will last almost indefinitely. Most pasta shapes can be substituted for one another, so I tend to keep one long shape and one short shape in the house and mix and match. If you enjoy Asian-style food, then pick up a package of rice noodles and also egg noodles so you can rustle up a quick salad or noodle soup any time.

I really enjoy using couscous for its "almost instant-ness," plus quinoa as a tasty and sustaining whole-grain for salads and pilafs. When making risottos, go for carnaroli rice if you can get it. Polenta should be the quick-cook variety for all recipes in this book. Look for it next to the dried pasta.

Flours & leavening (raising) agents
I've used all-purpose (plain) flour and baking powder mixed together in the baking recipes, as, depending on whether you live in the USA or Europe, self-rising (raising) flours are very different. American self-rising (raising) flour includes salt and I would not recommend it as a substitution. British self-raising (rising) flour can be substituted for the all-purpose (plain) flour in the baking recipes if you leave out the baking powder. The only recipe that this does not apply to is the Pistachio Yogurt Cake with Figs and Honey on page 298, where the weight of the nuts mean that you will still need to add 1 tsp baking powder if you are using self-rising flour. Modern milling techniques normally mean that you don't need to sift flour before using, but I still do it if the batter needs to be particularly light and airy, such as when

making scones. For bread making, choose extra-strong or bread flour and active dry (fast-action) yeast, which can be added straight to the flour without any fuss.

Ground or whole spices

I often use dried chili flakes, ground or whole cumin seeds, coriander, turmeric, chili powder, paprika (both smoked and ordinary), cinnamon, nutmeg, ginger, and fennel seed in this book. Try to buy spices in small quantities, as they lose their potency after a couple of months, and store them in a cool, dark place. Saffron is used a couple of times for its color and fragrance, but it is very expensive and can be omitted if necessary. Whole vanilla beans are ideal when you want to see flecks of vanilla as well as taste their superior flavor, but again expensive. You can use 1 teaspoon vanilla paste or 2 teaspoons extract in place of one bean.

Dried herbs

When fresh herbs aren't available, some dried herbs are helpful. Plus, some recipes are traditionally made with dried herbs, such as the fattoush salad on page 110. I use dried oregano and thyme most often in this book. Use 1 teaspoon dried herbs to every bunch of fresh where they can reasonably be substituted. For instance, dried rosemary would be fine for use in a marinade, but dried parsley wouldn't be right in a couscous salad.

Sugars & honey

Choose unrefined (golden) sugars for the best flavor. The most useful honey is the runny, clear type that can be measured from a squeezy bottle. You'll probably need to sift confectioners' (icing) sugar, and often brown sugars can be a bit lumpy, so give them a little rub through with your fingers if needed.

Dried fruit, nuts & seeds

Look for plump dried fruit. Good-quality brands tend to be juicier and nicer to eat in salads and so on. Nuts, especially ground nuts, can turn rancid within months, so don't stock up too much. Pine nuts are really quite pricey at the moment, so if you need to substitute almonds, then feel free. I like to use sesame seeds and sunflower seeds here and there, toasting them to bring out their taste. Why not toast a big batch, then keep in a sealed container, ready to use?

Mustards

Whole-grain and Dijon mustard are most commonly used for cooking as they have a gentle, rounded flavor. English mustard is more fiery. Buy English mustard powder if you can; then you have the choice of using it as part of a dry rub for the grill (barbecue), or mixing with water to serve as home-made mustard.

Garlic

Choose garlic with tight, papery and unblemished skin. I always go for bulbs with larger cloves.

Anchovies & capers

I prefer anchovies in oil and capers in brine, as they don't need to be rinsed before use, unlike those packed in salt.

Flavored oils

Sesame oil adds a rich nuttiness and walnut oil gives a lovely bittersweet flavor to salad dressings. This type of oil needs to be stored in a cool place away from direct light, as its flavor is easily impaired.

Salt & pepper

I like to use flaky Maldon sea salt and grind my own black peppercorns for maximum flavor and aroma. You could use any good-quality kosher or sea salt.

Vinegars

A bottle of good-quality white or red wine vinegar will last for months and give your salad dressings and sauces a wonderful piquancy. You'll find I've used cider vinegar and rice vinegar in some recipes when looking for a sweeter taste, but if you can't find or afford them, white wine vinegar and a pinch of sugar will do fine. Balsamic vinegar is sweet, normally a little thicker, and good for dressings, as well as cooking.

Broth (stock)

The better the broth, the better the end result. That said, broth made by dissolving a cube or powder in hot water is perfectly fine for adding to most recipes. Concentrated liquid broths will give a better result, but if you can, use good quality ready-made liquid broth (or even home-made) for meat gravies. This kind of broth will give gravies and soups great texture and flavor, as it will contain some of the natural gelatin from the bones from which it was made. If you choose to buy organic meat, then it makes sense to choose organic broth, too.

Sauces

Worcestershire sauce, soy sauce, Tabasco, and ketchup are all useful to have to hand, as are harissa or chili

paste. Fish sauce is essential for that authentic Thai taste.

Alcohol

A bottle of white wine or dry sherry is handy, but don't buy anything too expensive for cooking.

Time-saving items

Certain "cheat" ingredients make life easier and quicker, and although they often live in my fridge or freezer, I'd still call them pantry items. Ready-made bread crumbs can be frozen if you don't use them all. I turn to fresh ready-made pesto if I need to, and fresh filled pasta from the chilled aisle can be used in all sorts of ways. I tend to have a pot of low-fat yogurt ready most of the time, for dressings, marinades, dips, and tempering spicy food, plus a block of Parmesan for adding a bit of cheesy intensity here and there. I'll mention citrus fruits again here as I seem to reach for a lemon or a lime every time I cook in the warmer months, using the juice and zest as a seasoning for all sorts of salads, fish dishes, pastas, and desserts. Frozen peas and ready-made ice cream are also useful stand-bys.

BREAKFAST & BRUNCH

Bircher Muesli

Preparation time: 5 minutes,
plus soaking
Serves 4–6

If you're looking for a healthy but more exciting breakfast, try this super-easy soaked muesli. I've used raisins plus some apricots to add sweetness and texture, but if you'd rather use dates, dried apple, or whatever dried fruit is available, then feel free to throw them in. Top it off with fresh fruit and a drizzle of honey or maple syrup.

---

2 apples (choose a crisp, tangy
  variety such as Braeburn,
  Fuji, or Discovery)
scant 1½ cups (150 g) rolled oats
1¼ cups (300 g) plain yogurt
²/₃ cup (80 g) raisins, golden raisins
  or sultanas
¼ cup (50 g) dried apricots or
  peaches
²/₃ cup (150 ml) good-quality
  apple juice
a splash of milk, if needed
¾ cup (80 g) slivered (flaked)
  toasted almonds
1¾ cups (200 g) blueberries or other
  fresh fruit, to serve
maple syrup or honey, to serve
  (optional)

1
Coarsely grate the apples, without peeling first.

2
Put the apples, oats, yogurt, and raisins or sultanas into a medium bowl. With kitchen shears (scissors), snip in the dried apricots or peaches.

3
Add the apple juice, then stir well until evenly mixed. Cover the surface of the muesli with plastic wrap (clingfilm), then chill for at least 30 minutes or ideally overnight, which makes life easier in the morning.

4
Next day, give the muesli a stir. If it seems a bit thick, loosen with a splash of milk (or you can use more yogurt). Stir in most of the toasted nuts.

Spoon the muesli into bowls or glasses, top with the rest of the nuts and the berries, then drizzle with honey or maple syrup to your taste.

Avocado & Chorizo Toast

Preparation time: 5 minutes
Cooking time: 5 minutes
Serves 4

Wake up your taste buds with this fiery alternative to the sausage sandwich—my perfect food for the morning after the night before. The quality of the bread will really make all the difference here; you want something with a good chewy crust and character. If you can't find sourdough, then halve and toast some ciabatta or baguette instead.

---

9 oz (250 g) chorizo sausages

2 ripe avocados

4 scallions (spring onions)

2 limes

a few drops Tabasco sauce

1 tbsp extra-virgin olive oil, plus
    extra for drizzling

4 thick slices good-quality bread,
    such as sourdough

1 clove garlic

1 handful fresh cilantro (coriander)

sea salt and freshly ground
    black pepper

1
Cut the sausages into bite-size pieces. Heat a skillet or frying pan, add the sausages to the dry pan, then fry for 5 minutes, until golden and crisp around the edges. The sausages will release their own red oil as they cook.

CHORIZO
This piquant Spanish sausage is spiced with paprika and garlic, with a delicious smokiness. There are two types: cooking chorizo, which is soft like a regular sausage, and cured chorizo, which is firm and dry and eaten uncooked, like a salami. Either type will work in this recipe, but choose the cooking chorizo if you have the option.

2
Meanwhile, cut each avocado in half; then use a spoon to scoop out the pits (stones) and the flesh. Roughly slice or chop the flesh.

CHOOSING AND
PREPARING AVOCADOS
A ripe avocado will yield when gently pressed at the stalk end. Don't buy anything that feels mushy, as it will be past its best. An under-ripe avocado will soon ripen up in the fruit bowl or in a paper bag with an apple (apples release a gas that speeds up ripening). Store the ripe fruit in the fridge.

To cut an avocado in half, very carefully push the blade of a knife into the flesh, until the knife stops at the pit. Slide the knife all the way around the avocado, keeping the blade against the pit. Pull out the knife, then twist the 2 halves apart.

3

Thinly slice the scallions (spring onions) and squeeze the juice from one lime. Add the juice and onions to the avocados in a bowl. Add the Tabasco, and oil, then season to taste with salt and pepper. Cut the remaining lime into wedges.

4

Preheat the broiler (grill) and spread out the bread on a baking sheet. Toast until golden on both sides. Cut the garlic in half and rub the cut side over the toast. Drizzle with a little extra-virgin oil.

5

Top the toast with the avocado mixture, followed by the sizzling sausages and a spoonful of the cooking juices. Tear the cilantro (coriander) leaves over the top and serve with the extra lime wedges for squeezing.

Baked Eggs with Spinach & Feta

Preparation time: 20 minutes
Cooking time: 20 minutes
Serves 4

Eggs, spinach, and feta are great food friends and come together wonderfully in this delicious and veggie-friendly brunch. If you have some leftover potatoes in the fridge, then half the work has been done for you; simply wilt the spinach with boiling water from the kettle. Serve with bread, if you like.

---

11 oz (300 g) new potatoes

1 clove garlic

9 oz (250 g) baby spinach

1¼ cups (300 ml) pureed canned
  tomatoes (passata)

½ tsp hot smoked paprika, plus
  a little pinch for sprinkling

4 eggs

2 tbsp (25 g) butter, chilled

2 oz (50 g) feta cheese

good crusty bread, to serve
  (optional)

sea salt and freshly ground
  black pepper

1

Preheat the oven to 400°F (200°C/
Gas Mark 6). Cut the potatoes
into chunky pieces, then put them
into a medium pan and cover with
cold water. Bring to a boil, then
boil for 10–15 minutes, until tender.

2

While you wait for the potatoes to
boil, thinly slice the garlic. Rinse
the spinach in a bowl of cold water,
then lift it into a colander and drain.

WASHING LEAFY VEGETABLES
Spinach can be a bit gritty, so it's
always best to give it a good wash.
As the leaves float around, the dirt
sinks to the bottom of the bowl.
Lift them out of the water rather
than pouring the dirty water back
over the leaves as you drain. This
method is useful for washing herbs
and other leafy vegetables too.

3

When the potatoes are tender, drain
them over the spinach. The hot water
will wilt the leaves.

4
Transfer the potatoes from the colander into 2 shallow ovenproof dishes. Squeeze as much liquid from the spinach as you can with the back of a wooden spoon. Season with salt and pepper.

5
Scatter the spinach over the potatoes, then spoon the pureed canned tomatoes (passata) over them and sprinkle with the garlic. Season with salt and pepper and the ½ teaspoon smoked paprika. Make 2 wells in the vegetables, so that the eggs have somewhere to sit.

6
Crack an egg into each well, then season the tops with a sprinkling of extra paprika, salt, and pepper. Cut the butter into little pieces and dot it over everything.

7
Put the dishes onto a baking sheet. Bake for 15–20 minutes, until the eggs are just set and the tomatoes are bubbling around the edges. The eggs will continue to cook once they come out of the oven, so don't be worried if the whites still look a little runny. Crumble the cheese over the top, then serve hot with bread, if you like.

Blueberry & Cream Cheese Muffins

Preparation time: 15 minutes, plus cooling
Cooking time: 18–20 minutes
Makes 12

A tray of muffins is always a welcome sight. The cream cheese is a tasty optional extra and contrasts well with the sweetness of the blueberries. Try using the basic recipe with other fruit: chopped fresh peach or plum would work just as nicely.

---

7 tbsp (100 g) unsalted butter

3 tbsp sunflower or vegetable oil

1 cup (250 g) low-fat plain yogurt
  (or you can use buttermilk)

2 tsp vanilla extract

3 eggs

3¼ cups (375 g) all-purpose
  (plain) flour

1 tbsp baking powder

¼ tsp fine salt

1 scant cup (200 g) superfine
  (caster) sugar

6 oz (175 g) blueberries

4 oz (120 g) cream cheese

1

Melt the butter in a medium pan. While you wait, line a 12-cup muffin pan with muffin wrappers (cases) and preheat the oven to 400°F (200°C/Gas Mark 6), setting a rack in the middle of the oven.

2

Whisk the oil, yogurt, vanilla, and eggs into the butter, in that order.

3

Sift the flour and baking powder into a large mixing bowl, stir in the salt and sugar, then make a well in the middle.

4

Pour the yogurt mixture into the mixing bowl. Fold the dry ingredients into the wet using a rubber spatula, but take great care not to overstir as this can make the muffins tough. When most of the mixture has come together, but you can still see large ribbons of flour, stop. Pour in the blueberries, then fold them into the batter with the bare minimum of stirring. The mixture will still look lumpy and uneven.

5

Using 2 dessertspoons, spoon about half of the batter into the prepared pan. Now dot about ½ teaspoon of the cheese on top of each half-filled muffin. Top with the rest of the batter (the wrappers will be quite full), then top each one with another ½ teaspoon of cheese. I always try and engineer it so that there are a few berries on the top of the muffin batter so they look really blueberry-ish when they come out of the oven.

6

Bake the muffins for 18–20 minutes, or until well risen and golden and the blueberries are starting to ooze their purple juices. Let cool in the pan for 10 minutes, then transfer to a cooling rack and let cool completely. Muffins are always best enjoyed on the day they're made—or kept in an airtight container overnight.

Breakfast Blinis with Smoked Salmon

Preparation time: 15 minutes
Cooking time: less than 10 minutes
Serves 4

Buckwheat flour gives a light nuttiness to these pancakes. A traditional blini would be made with yeast, but baking powder is a lot simpler and quicker to use. Have all your prep done before you cook the pancakes so you're free to eat them fresh from the pan and at their best.

1 bunch fresh dill

3½ oz (100 g) wild arugula (rocket)

½ red onion

1 lemon

⅔ cup (150 g) crème fraîche
   or thick sour cream

2 tbsp (25 g) unsalted butter

1¾ cups (200 g) buckwheat flour

2 tsp baking powder

½ tsp fine salt

3 eggs

1¼ cups (300 ml) buttermilk or
   low-fat plain yogurt

2–3 tbsp vegetable or sunflower oil,
   for frying

7 oz (200 g) smoked salmon

1 tbsp capers in brine, drained

sea salt and freshly ground
   black pepper

1

Finely chop the dill and half of the arugula (rocket). Finely chop the onion.

2

Cut the lemon into wedges. Mix the crème fraîche or sour cream with a squeeze of lemon, then add half of the dill and season with salt and pepper.

3

Melt the butter in a pan, or in a microwavable bowl.

4

Put the flour, baking powder, and salt into a large bowl. Crack the eggs into the bowl, then add the buttermilk and melted butter.

BUCKWHEAT FLOUR

Buckwheat isn't actually wheat, but a seed. The seeds are ground to make a nutty, grayish flour that is naturally gluten-free. Buckwheat grows well in harsh climates and soils too poor to sustain other cereal crops. It has been an important source of nutrition for centuries, used to make pancakes, noodles, pastas, and cereals. Find it in the baking or special diets area of larger supermarkets. A mixture of half whole-grain (wholewheat) and half all-purpose (plain) flour makes a good substitute.

5

Using a balloon whisk, beat the ingredients until smooth and thick. Add the remaining chopped dill and chopped arugula.

6

When you're ready to cook, put the oven on low. Set a large nonstick skillet or frying pan over a medium heat. Add a splash of the oil, then add three large spoonfuls of the batter. The batter should sizzle gently as it settles into the oil. Cook until you can see bubbles appear on the surface and a tinge of gold around the edge of each blini.

7

Flip the blinis carefully using a spatula (fish slice), then cook for another minute or so, until puffed up in the middle and golden on both sides. Keep the first few batches warm in the oven while you make the rest, adding a little more oil to the pan each time.

8

To serve, arrange the slices of salmon on the blinis, spoon the dill cream over the salmon and sprinkle with the capers and onions. Serve with the remaining arugula leaves and a lemon wedge for squeezing.

Zingy Fruit Salad

Preparation time: 5–10 minutes
Serves 4

We can all chop up a bit of fruit and call it fruit salad. But love it a little, dress it just as you would a regular salad (in this case with fresh lime), and yours will be in a whole different league. Feel free to change the fruit to whatever soft or stone fruit is in season near you, although I would always keep the banana in there, for both its sweetness and energy-boosting qualities.

---

a few black peppercorns (optional)

2 limes

1–2 tbsp superfine (caster) sugar, depending on your taste

1 mcdium ripe melon, about 2¼ lb (1 kg), at room temperature

3½ cups (400 g) ripe strawberries, at room temperature

2 just-ripe bananas

1 small handful fresh mint

4 tbsp coconut milk or cream (optional)

1

Crush the peppercorns in a mortar with a pestle. Squeeze the limes and mix the juice with the sugar and pepper, stirring until the sugar has dissolved.

JUICING CITRUS FRUIT
Some citrus fruit can be almost juiceless. Often I blast limes and lemons in the microwave for a few seconds before juicing—this seems to loosen everything up a little inside. Always choose fruit that feels heavy for its size.

2

Cut the melon in half, scoop out the seeds with a spoon, then cut into wedges. Cut vertical slits into each wedge, then run the knife between the flesh and the skin to release the slices.

3

Add the melon to the lime syrup. Cut the tops from the strawberries, then cut the berries in half, or into quarters if large. Mix into the melon. The salad can be made up to 12 hours ahead and kept covered in the fridge at this point, if you like.

THINK TEMPERATURE
Excess cold will deaden the taste of your fruit salad, so it's vital to let the melon and strawberries come to life a little out of the fridge before making it. If you want to make the salad ahead, then take it out of the fridge 30 minutes before you want to serve.

4

When ready to serve, peel and slice the bananas and add to the salad. Pick the mint leaves from the stems and tear into the bowl. Toss well.

5

Serve the salad and the juice in bowls, then spoon over a little coconut milk or cream, if using.

Asparagus & Bacon Frittata

Preparation time: 5 minutes
Cooking time: about 15 minutes
Serves 4

Eggs, bacon, tomatoes—almost all the elements of a classic breakfast, but shaken up with a fresh blast of basil pesto and seasonal green vegetables. Add a handful of sliced mushrooms to the bacon if you like. If there are any leftovers (I doubt it), pack them into lunchboxes. Enjoy with good crusty bread.

---

6 strips (rashers) bacon
   (dry-cured is best)
5 oz (150 g) asparagus
1 handful cherry tomatoes
8 eggs
2 tbsp fresh pesto from the
   refrigerated aisle of your
   supermarket
extra-virgin olive oil, for drizzling
sea salt and freshly ground
   black pepper
good-quality bread for serving
   (optional)

1

With kitchen shears (scissors), snip the bacon into bite-size pieces. Heat an 8-inch (20-cm) skillet or frying pan, then add the bacon and cook for 5 minutes, or until golden and the fat has started to run.

2

Meanwhile, cut the bottom 2 inches (5 cm) from each asparagus spear, as the ends can often be a bit tough. Cut the spears into shorter lengths, and cut the cherry tomatoes in half.

3

Preheat the broiler (grill). Lift the bacon onto a plate and spoon off the excess fat, leaving about 1 tablespoon behind in the pan. Add the asparagus to the pan and fry it for 3 minutes, or until bright green and just tender to the bite (try a bit if you're not sure, and remember it is going to cook more once the eggs are added).

4

Beat the eggs together. Season with pepper, but take it easy with the salt as the bacon will add plenty. Return the bacon to the pan, then pour in the eggs. Turn the heat down to low.

5

Cook the frittata for 5 minutes, or until the eggs are nearly set. Stir the eggs around very gently a few times as they cook, letting the liquid egg fill the gaps that the spoon makes.

6

When the eggs are almost set, scatter with the cherry tomatoes, spoon dollops of pesto over the top, then season with salt and pepper.

CHOOSING PESTOS
Pesto from the refrigerated aisle has a fresher basil and Parmesan flavor than pesto sold in a jar. It does cost more, but the taste is worth it. Alternatively, you could add fresh chopped basil to jarred pesto, or make a batch yourself. Simply put 3 oz (80 g) toasted pine nuts (or almonds), 1 clove garlic, 1 large bunch of basil and ⅔ cup (150 ml) olive oil into a food processor and pulse to a paste. Stir in 2 oz (50 g) finely grated Parmesan cheese. Chill for up to a week and use for pasta and soups.

7

Put the pan under the broiler for just a few minutes, until the eggs are set and the top is turning golden. Serve cut into wedges, with a drizzle of extra-virgin olive oil and some good bread, if you like.

Sticky Fig & Ricotta Toast

Preparation time: 5 minutes
Cooking time: 5 minutes
Serves 4, easily halved

Another great little breakfast that
looks stunning but is simplicity itself
to make. The maple and cinnamon
infused figs are also good enjoyed
as dessert, either warm or cold, with
thick yogurt.

8 ripe figs

1 handful whole almonds

2 tbsp (25 g) unsalted butter

1 tsp ground cinnamon

4 tbsp maple syrup or honey

4 thick slices good-quality
   fruit bread

9 oz (250 g) ricotta cheese

1

Preheat the broiler (grill). Trim the stems from the figs if necessary, then cut an "X" through each fig going almost all the way to the bottom. Open the fruit out a little, like a flower. Very roughly chop the almonds.

2

Put the figs into a medium baking dish. Add a little dot of butter to the middle of each fig, then sprinkle with cinnamon and drizzle the maple syrup or honey over the tops.

3
Broil (grill) the figs for about
5 minutes, or until softened but not
collapsed, and surrounded with
a delicious cinnamon butter syrup.

4
Let the figs cool for a few minutes.
While you wait, spread out the
bread on a baking sheet and toast
under the broiler. Add the nuts to
the baking sheet when you toast the
second side of the bread.

5
Spread the ricotta over the toast,
then top with the figs and nuts and
spoonfuls of the warm syrup.

QUICK LUNCHES & SUPPERS

Grilled Halloumi with Pomegranate Tabbouleh

Preparation time: 15 minutes
Cooking time: 5 minutes
Serves 4, easily doubled or more

Tabbouleh is a fresh, lively Middle Eastern salad of chopped herbs with plenty of lemon and bulgur wheat, and here I've added chickpeas to make it extra sustaining. The salad is also delicious with goat cheese, fish, grilled meat, and hummus, among other things.

---

²/₃ cup (120 g) bulgur wheat
2²/₃ cups (400 ml) hot vegetable
   broth (stock)
2 organic (unwaxed) lemons
3 tbsp extra-virgin olive oil, plus
   extra to drizzle (optional)
1 large bunch fresh flat-leaf parsley
1 large bunch fresh mint
1 bunch scallions (spring onions)
14 oz (400 g) canned chickpeas,
   drained
½ cup (100 g) pomegranate seeds
1 lb 2 oz (500 g) halloumi cheese
sea salt and freshly ground
   black pepper

1
Put the bulgur wheat into a large bowl. Pour in the hot broth (stock), then cover the bowl and let stand for 15 minutes.

2
While you wait, finely grate the zest from the lemons, then squeeze the juice from 1 (about 3 tablespoons). Whisk the zest and juice with the olive oil and some salt and pepper.

3
Pick the parsley and mint leaves from the stems, then finely chop. Trim and thinly slice the scallions (spring onions).

BULGUR WHEAT
Bulgur wheat is part-ground, part-cooked wheat that's really healthy and quick to use and has a more interesting texture than couscous. If you can't find bulgur, use couscous instead, adding enough hot broth to just cover the surface. Alternatively, the salad could easily be made with cooked quinoa, rice, or any other grains.

4

Drain the bulgur in a strainer (sieve), then return to the bowl. Add the dressing, herbs, onions, chickpeas, and most of the pomegranate seeds. Stir well and season to taste with salt and pepper.

5

When you're ready to serve, heat a ridged grill pan (griddle). Cut the halloumi into slices about ½-inch (1-cm) thick. Cook the cheese for 2 minutes on each side, or until it comes away easily from the ridges of the pan. A frosting spatula (palette knife) will be handy to lift and turn the cheese. If you don't have a grill pan, just brown the halloumi in a dry skillet or frying pan instead.

6

Spoon the salad onto serving plates, top with the cheese, then sprinkle with the rest of the pomegranate seeds. Serve with a wedge of lemon and a drizzle more oil, if you like.

Creamy Zucchini, Lemon, & Pea Pasta

Preparation time: 10 minutes
Cooking time: 10 minutes
Serves 2, easily doubled

You'll probably have most of the ingredients for this fresh pasta in the pantry (storecupboard) and freezer already, so just head to the store for the zucchini (courgettes) and crème fraîche and you're 20 minutes away from a delicious supper. A few strips of crisp bacon or a few chili flakes would be a nice addition, too.

---

7 oz (200 g) spaghetti

2 zucchini (courgettes), about
   9 oz (250 g) in total

1 tbsp extra-virgin olive oil

1 small clove garlic

1 egg

scant ½ cup (100 g) crème fraîche
   or sour cream

1 organic (unwaxed) lemon

1 oz (25 g) Parmesan cheese

3½ oz (100 g) frozen peas

sea salt and freshly ground
   black pepper

1

Bring a large pan of salted water to a boil. Add the spaghetti, then, once it has collapsed into the water, stir and let boil for 8 minutes.

2

While the pasta cooks, chop the zucchini (courgettes) into cubes, or just slice into ½-inch (1-cm) rounds. Heat the oil in a large skillet or frying pan, then add the zucchini.

3

Cook for 4–5 minutes, stirring often, until golden and tender. Crush the garlic, stir it into the zucchini and cook for another 1–2 minutes, until it has softened.

4

Separate the egg, putting the yolk into a small bowl.

SEPARATING AN EGG
Gently crack the shell against the side of a small bowl. Slowly pull the shell apart as cleanly as possible along the crack, tipping the yolk into one half of the shell. Let the white drain away into a bowl below. Drop the yolk into another small bowl.

5

Add the crème fraîche or sour cream to the egg yolk, then finely grate in the lemon zest. Squeeze the lemon, then add 1 tablespoon juice to the bowl. Finely grate the cheese and stir most of it into the mixture, along with some salt and pepper.

6

When the pasta has cooked for 8 minutes, add the peas and bring the pan back to a boil. By this time the peas should be tender and the pasta al dente (see below). Reserve a cupful of the cooking water, then drain the pasta and peas in a colander.

IS MY PASTA COOKED?
Forget flinging a piece onto the wall to see if it sticks. The easiest way to tell if pasta is cooked is to bite it. It should be tender, but with the slightest resistance in the middle— *al dente*—neither chewy nor soggy.

7

Return the pasta to its pan (off the heat), then add the zucchini and the creamy sauce. Spoon in 5 tablespoons of the cooking water, then toss everything together well until coated and creamy. Taste for seasoning and add more salt, pepper, or lemon juice if you need to.

8

Serve the pasta in bowls, sprinkled with the rest of the Parmesan.

Carrot Falafel with Sesame Sauce

Preparation time: 15 minutes
Cooking time: under 15 minutes
Serves 4, easily doubled

The great thing about falafel (apart from being good for you, easy, and filling) is that they reheat wonderfully or can be eaten cold, so you can make a batch and let the family enjoy them whenever it suits. Try as a lunchbox filler with a pot of hummus and some vegetable sticks to make a change from the usual sandwiches.

2 cloves garlic

1 bunch fresh flat-leaf parsley

1 tbsp ground cumin

1 tbsp ground coriander

½ tsp dried crushed chiles
   or chili powder

14 oz (400 g) canned chickpeas,
   drained

1 egg

2 carrots

1 organic (unwaxed) lemon

1 tbsp olive oil

⅔ cup (150 g) plain yogurt

1 tbsp tahini (sesame seed paste)

1 red onion

1 handful fresh mint

whole-grain (wholemeal) tortillas
   or pita bread

sea salt and freshly ground
   black pepper

pickled chiles, to serve (optional)

1
Coarsely chop the garlic and parsley, including the parsley stems. Put into a food processor with the spices, chickpeas, and egg.

2
Pulse the mixer to make a finely chopped and fairly dry-looking mixture. If you don't have a processor, mash the chickpeas with a potato masher and finely chop the garlic and herbs, then combine.

3
Coarsely grate the carrots and finely grate the zest of the lemon. Scoop the falafel mixture into a bowl, then add the carrots and lemon zest. Season to taste with salt and pepper.

4
Stir to combine, then shape the mixture into about 12 patties, pressing the mixture firmly together with cupped hands. The falafel can be kept in the fridge for up to 24 hours, if you'd like to get ahead.

5

Heat a little oil in a nonstick skillet or frying pan, then cook the falafel in batches for about 3 minutes on each side, until golden. Don't be tempted to add more oil, as this can cause the patties to break up.

6

Squeeze the juice from the lemon. Whisk together the yogurt, tahini and 1 tablespoon lemon juice until smooth and spoonable. Add a little water if it's a bit too thick. Season to taste with salt and pepper, and more lemon juice if you like.

7

Thinly slice the red onion and pick the mint leaves from their stems. Toss with the remaining lemon juice and season with salt and pepper.

8

Warm the tortillas or pita breads in the microwave or in a hot pan according to the package instructions, then serve topped with the falafel, sesame yogurt, onion salad, and pickled chiles.

Spicy Shrimp (Prawn), Fennel, & Chile Linguine

Preparation time: 10 minutes
Cooking time: 15 minutes
Serves 2, easily doubled

This recipe is a regular in my home all year round. In the winter I brown good sausage meat instead of the shrimp (prawns), then simmer the sauce with canned tomatoes.

6 oz (175 g) linguine (or any other
   long pasta shape)
1 large or 2 smaller fennel bulbs
2 tbsp extra-virgin olive oil,
   plus extra for drizzling
2 cloves garlic
1 fat red chile
1 lemon
¼ tsp fennel seeds (optional)
3½ oz (100 g) cherry tomatoes
7 oz (200 g) large, uncooked peeled
   shrimp (prawns), thawed if frozen
1 handful fresh flat-leaf parsley
sea salt and freshly ground
   black pepper

1
Bring a large pan of salted water to a boil. Add the pasta, then once it has collapsed into the water, stir it and let boil for 8–10 minutes, until just tender.

IS MY PASTA COOKED?
Forget flinging a piece onto the wall to see if it sticks. The easiest way to tell if pasta is cooked is to bite it. It should be tender, but with the slightest resistance in the middle—*al dente*—neither chewy nor soggy.

2
While the pasta cooks, cut the fennel bulb in half and remove any very tough outer layers. You can also remove the core if you like. Thinly slice the fennel. Reserve the feathery leaves, if there are any.

3
Heat the oil in a large skillet or frying pan, then add the fresh fennel. Cook for 10 minutes over medium heat, stirring often, until softened and sweet and turning golden in places.

DEFROSTING FROZEN
SHRIMP (PRAWNS)
To defrost frozen shrimp quickly, put them into a large bowl and cover with cold water. Leave for a few minutes, then drain off the water and repeat. Pat dry and use immediately.

4

While you wait, thinly slice the garlic and chile. Deseed the chile first if you like. The easiest way to do this is by scraping out the middle with a teaspoon. Coarsely chop the parsley leaves and cut the lemon into quarters.

HOW HOT IS YOUR CHILE?
To avoid spoiling a dish with too much or little chile, taste a tiny bit first or touch the cut edge of the chile with a finger and test the juice. If it's mild, add more, if it's too fiery, add less.

5

Add the garlic, chile, fennel seeds, if using, and cherry tomatoes to the pan. Cook for 2 minutes or until fragrant and the tomato skins are starting to pop. Now add the shrimp and cook for about 3 minutes or until the shrimp have changed color all the way through.

6

Reserve a cup of the pasta cooking water, then drain the pasta in a colander.

7

Add the pasta, 5 tablespoons of the cooking water, the parsley and any fennel leaves to the shrimp pan, then squeeze in the juice from 2 of the lemon wedges. Season generously with salt and pepper and toss everything together. Adjust the taste by adding more lemon juice, salt and pepper if needed. Serve drizzled with a little more oil and the remaining lemon wedges for squeezing.

Asparagus & Poached Egg with Balsamic Butter

Preparation time: 10 minutes
Cooking time: 10 minutes
Serves 2, easily doubled or more

Most recipes for asparagus will involve steaming or boiling but I love to cook it in a pan or grill pan (griddle) or even roast it. Prepared this way the asparagus retains all of its freshness, and it's harder to overcook. For best results, buy the asparagus on the day of eating and look for firm, perky green spears.

9 oz (250 g) asparagus
chunk of Parmesan cheese,
    for shaving
1 tbsp white wine vinegar
2 eggs, as fresh as possible
1 tbsp sunflower or vegetable oil
2 tbsp (25 g) unsalted butter
1 tsp balsamic vinegar
sea salt and freshly ground
    black pepper

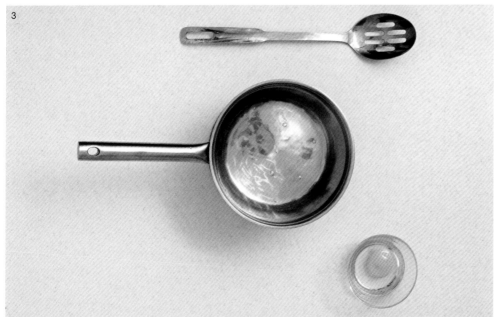

1
Cut the bottom 2 inches (5 cm) from each asparagus spear, as the ends can often be a bit tough.

2
Using a vegetable peeler, peel a handful of Parmesan shavings from the block.

3
Bring a deep pan of water to a boil, then add the wine vinegar and season generously with salt. Break 1 egg into a small bowl or cup. When boiling, stir the water with a slotted spoon to make a whirlpool.

4
Gently slide the egg into the middle of the swirling water. Turn the heat to a simmer and cook the egg gently for 3 minutes, or until the white and yolk have set. Meanwhile, break the second egg into the bowl or cup.

5

Lift the egg from the pan with the slotted spoon, then transfer it to a bowl of hot (not boiling) water. This will keep it warm while you poach the second egg.

6

While the second egg simmers, start cooking the asparagus. Heat a large skillet or frying pan over high heat, then add the oil. Add the asparagus, season with salt and pepper, and cook for 3–5 minutes, depending on the thickness of the spears. Toss the spears frequently, until golden in places and just tender to the bite.

7

Take the pan from the heat and let it cool for a few seconds. Add the butter and balsamic vinegar and let the butter melt.

8

Lift the asparagus onto warmed serving plates, then spoon over some of the balsamic butter. Drain the eggs (pat dry underneath with a little paper towel or a clean dish towel), then place one on top of each mound of asparagus. Scatter the Parmesan shavings over the plates. Sprinkle the eggs with salt and pepper and serve.

Chicken & Blue Cheese Waldorf Salad

Preparation time: 10 minutes
Cooking time: 10 minutes
Serves 2, easily doubled

I often cook chicken breasts this way, butterflied out to cut the cooking time. To make this recipe even quicker, strip the meat from a small rotisserie chicken and use that instead of grilling your own. The blue cheese adds another tangy dimension to this classic salad and marries perfectly with grapes, chicken, and celery.

---

2 skinless, boneless chicken breasts

olive oil, for rubbing

1 small handful pecan halves

2 stems celery

½ apple, preferably tangy and
    red-skinned, such as Braeburn

1 handful black or red
    seedless grapes

½ small red onion

1½ oz (40 g) creamy blue cheese
    (optional)

2 tbsp mayonnaise

2 tbsp plain yogurt

1 tsp white wine vinegar

3½ oz (100 g) watercress or
    another peppery green
    such as arugula (rocket)

sea salt and freshly ground
    black pepper

1
Heat a ridged grill pan (griddle) or nonstick skillet (frying pan). Slice the chicken across the middle, opening each breast out into a heart shape.

2
Season the chicken well on both sides with salt and pepper, rub with a little oil, then put into the hot pan. Cook on the first side for 5 minutes, until striped and golden underneath. Turn the chicken over, add the pecans to the pan and cook for another 5 minutes, stirring the nuts around now and again. The chicken is ready when it feels firm to the touch, all signs of pink have disappeared, and any juices run clear. Lift the chicken out of the pan and set the toasted nuts aside.

3

While the chicken cooks, start assembling the salad. Thinly slice the celery and apple, halve the grapes and finely chop the onion. Put into a large bowl, then crumble in the blue cheese, if using.

4

Whisk the mayonnaise, yogurt and vinegar together and season to taste with salt and pepper to make a dressing. Whisk in any resting juices from the chicken too.

5

Stir the dressing into the salad and add the pecans. This can be made up to a day in advance, if you want to get ahead.

6

Slice the chicken thickly. Spread out the watercress over 2 plates. Top with the creamy salad and the juicy chicken, then serve immediately.

Tortellini Soup

Preparation time: 10 minutes
Cooking time: less than 20 minutes
Serves 4, easily doubled

A sort of super summer minestrone, this ultra-easy soup is healthy and quick. If you want to shave even more time from the cooking, the tomatoes can be replaced with a can of drained plum tomatoes (just mash them up in the pan). The caper and parsley mixture gives a vibrant shot of herby deliciousness to each bowl.

2 slim leeks

6 tbsp extra-virgin olive oil

2 zucchini (courgettes)

1 clove garlic

11 oz (300 g) ripe tomatoes

1 bunch fresh flat-leaf parsley

1½ tbsp capers in brine, drained

3¼ cups (800 ml) chicken or
    vegetable broth (stock)

9 oz (250 g) filled pasta shapes
    (I used cheese and ham tortellini)

sea salt and freshly ground
    black pepper

1

Trim and discard the tough green parts from the leeks, then slice the pale green and white parts into thin rounds. Heat 2 tablespoons of the oil in a large pan and add the leeks to give them a slight head start. Chop the zucchini (courgettes) into cubes or rounds, then stir into the pan. Season generously with salt and pepper. Cook the vegetables for 10 minutes, until just tender.

2

While you're waiting, crush the garlic and add it to the pan.Coarsely chop the tomatoes, removing any tough green stalky bits. Finely chop the parsley leaves and capers, then mix in a small bowl with the remaining oil and some salt and pepper.

3

When the vegetables have softened, add the tomatoes to the pan. Simmer for a couple of minutes, until the tomatoes have released their juice and are starting to look pulpy.

4

Pour the broth (stock) over the vegetables, bring to a boil, then add the pasta shapes and boil for 2 minutes or until the pasta is just cooked through (the cooking time may differ so check the package instructions).

5

Season the soup to taste, then ladle into bowls. Serve with a spoonful of the parsley and caper sauce.

Peach & Mozzarella Platter

Preparation time: less than 10 minutes
Serves 2, easily doubled or more

When fuzzy peaches are at their aromatic best, why save them for dessert? Served with salty cured ham, creamy cheese, and balsamic vinegar, they make one of the best lazy suppers going. Let the fruit come up to room temperature before preparing—the taste will be more rounded and the texture softer.

---

2 ripe peaches or nectarines

4 slices prosciutto, Serrano or
    other tasty cured ham

1 x 8-oz (225-g) ball buffalo
    mozzarella, drained

1 handful fresh basil

2 tsp balsamic vinegar, or more
    to taste

a little extra-virgin olive oil

freshly ground black pepper

good crusty bread, to serve
    (optional)

1

Run your knife around each peach, then twist in half and remove the pits (stones). Cut the flesh into wedges.

PREPARING STONE FRUIT
Sometimes removing pits from peaches and other stone fruit (plums, cherries) is easy, sometimes not. It's all down to whether the fruit is "clingstone" or "freestone". As you'd expect, clingstone peaches have flesh that clings to the stone and freestone fruit comes away easily. There's no real way to tell them apart when buying, but if you end up with cling then don't worry—just cut the fruit away in large pieces instead.

2

Spread the peaches over a large plate. Tear the ham a little, then arrange it around and over the fruit.

3

Tear the mozzarella over the peaches and ham in rough chunks or ribbons.

CHOOSING MOZZARELLA
As this will be eaten more or less unadulterated, quality is all-important, so make sure that you get the best buffalo mozzarella you can for this recipe. Save the cheaper cow milk mozzarella for topping pizzas or baked pasta.

4

Sprinkle with the basil leaves, the balsamic vinegar, and a little oil, then season with plenty of black pepper. Enjoy the salad as soon as you have dressed it, perhaps with good crusty bread.

Chicken & Ham Parmesan

Preparation time: 15 minutes
Cooking time: 15–20 minutes
Serves 4

The whole family will enjoy sharing this good old classic. Rather than coating the chicken in crumbs and pan-frying it, I just top it with cheesy crumbs and bake. The tomato sauce is rich, thick and super-simple to make. Use it on pasta or to serve with simply cooked steak, chicken, or chops.

2 cloves garlic

11 oz (300 g) ripe tomatoes

1 bunch fresh basil

3 tbsp extra-virgin olive oil

2 tbsp tomato pastc (purée)

1 tsp superfine (caster) sugar

½ cup (25 g) fresh white
    bread crumbs

1 oz (25 g) chunk Parmesan or other
    tasty, mature hard cheese

1 x 4-oz (120-g) ball buffalo
    mozzarella, drained

4 skinless, boneless chicken breasts

4 slices smoked ham, not too thick

sea salt and freshly ground
    black pepper

green salad and crusty bread, to
    serve (optional)

1

Start the tomato sauce first. Crush or finely slice the garlic and roughly chop the tomatoes and most of the basil leaves.

2

Heat 2 tablespoons of the oil in an ovenproof skillet, frying pan, or Dutch oven (casserole dish), then add the garlic. Cook for 1 minute, until softened but not golden, then add the tomatoes and chopped basil. Stir in the tomato paste (purée) and sugar.

3

Simmer the sauce for a couple of minutes until the tomatoes are softened and the sauce is rich and thick. Season to taste with salt and pepper.

4

Preheat the oven to 375°F (190°C/ Gas Mark 5). Mix the crumbs, Parmesan, and the rest of the oil. Cut the mozzarella into 8 slices.

5

Slice the chicken through the side of each breast, cutting almost all the way through but not quite, then open out to make a heart shape. Season the chicken with pepper, place a folded slice of ham on the righthand side of each breast, then top with a piece of mozzarella. Fold over the lefthand side of the chicken to close.

6

Sit the chicken in the tomato sauce (spoon the sauce into a baking dish if the pan isn't ovenproof). Top the chicken with the remaining mozzarella and sprinkle with the cheesy crumbs. The whole dish can be covered, then chilled for up to a day if you want to get ahead.

7

Bake the chicken for 15–20 minutes or until golden on top and the cheese is melting in the middle. Let the dish sit for a few minutes to let the chicken rest a little, then scatter with the remaining basil leaves and serve with a salad and crusty bread.

Vietnamese Herb &
Noodle Salad

Preparation time: 10 minutes
Serves 2, easily doubled

Fresh Vietnamese summer rolls are
ideal summer food but unless you
live near an Asian supermarket, the
rice paper wrappers can be very
tricky to find. This recipe includes
almost all of the same ingredients,
but uses rice noodles instead of
the wrappers. The salad goes
wonderfully with shredded cooked
chicken and pork too.

2 oz (50 g) thin or thick rice noodles

½ cucumber

2 carrots

1 handful fresh mint

1 handful fresh cilantro (coriander)

1 lime

1 tbsp fish sauce

1 tbsp light brown (light
    muscovado) sugar

1 small hot red or green chile

1 clove garlic

½ smallish head iceberg lettuce

5 oz (150 g) whole cooked large
    shrimp (prawns)

1

Boil a kettle of water. Put the noodles into a large heatproof bowl and pour plenty of just-boiled water over them to cover. Let stand for 5 minutes, until softened and just tender. Thinner noodles take less time than thicker ones so check the package instructions.

RICE NOODLES

Rice noodles are all about texture. Made with rice flour, these slippery white noodles have a light, barely there flavor that will happily take on most Asian sauces and dressings and can also be used in soups. They vary from very fine to wide ribbons and most just need a quick soaking, or can be added at the very end of cooking (check the package first). To prepare ahead, drain, rinse and drain again, then run a little oil through the strands to keep them separated.

2

Prepare the vegetables while you wait. Thinly slice the cucumber, then cut into sticks. Coarsely grate or shred the carrots. Pick the leaves from the mint and the cilantro (coriander). Tear any larger mint leaves.

3

Squeeze the lime juice and mix with the fish sauce and sugar. Thinly slice the chile and crush the garlic, then add to the mixture.

4

Thinly shred the lettuce.

5

Drain the noodles in a strainer (sieve). If you are concerned that they might be starting to stick together, rinse them under cold running water and let drain.

6

Toss the vegetables, noodles, herbs, and shrimp (prawns) together, then drizzle with the dressing to serve.

Chipotle Chicken Fajitas

Preparation time: 10 minutes
Cooking time: 10 minutes
Serves 4, easily halved

Hot, tasty, and superfast, fajitas make great family food for busy weeknights. It's tempting to overfill the tortillas but to avoid getting messy, think less is more—you can always roll another. To make burritos in advance, see the tip on page 94.

2 bell peppers

1 onion

1 tbsp olive or vegetable oil

3–4 chicken breasts

1 bunch fresh cilantro (coriander)

1 tbsp cumin seeds

1 tbsp chipotle paste

1 tbsp tomato paste (purée)

1 tsp superfine (caster) sugar

3 oz (80 g) hard, tasty cheese,
    such as mature Cheddar

½–⅔ cup (125–150 ml) sour cream

6–8 flour tortillas

sea salt and freshly ground
    black pepper

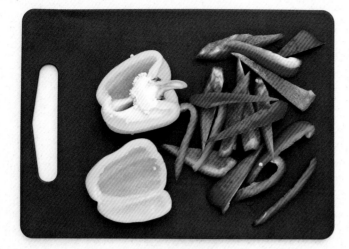

1

2

3

1

Deseed, then slice the bell peppers into chunky strips. Slice the onion.

PREPARING BELL PEPPERS
Cut the bell pepper in half through the stalk. Carefully run your knife around the top of the bell pepper to remove the stalk and the majority of the seeds. Trim away any remaining white membrane before slicing the flesh.

2

Heat a large skillet or frying pan over medium heat. Add a splash of oil, wait a few seconds, then add the peppers and onions. Cook, stirring frequently, for 5 minutes, or until starting to soften and turn golden at the edges.

3

While you wait, cut the chicken into finger-width strips and put into a large bowl. Finely chop the cilantro (coriander) stems, then add to the chicken, along with the cumin seeds and some salt and pepper. Stir until the chicken is evenly coated.

4

Transfer the cooked vegetables to a plate or bowl, add another splash of oil to the pan, then cook the chicken for 5 minutes, stirring frequently, until golden and just cooked through.

5

While the chicken cooks, make the sauce. Stir together the chipotle paste, tomato paste (purée), and sugar, then season with salt and pepper. Loosen with 2 tablespoons of water or until the sauce is the consistency of ketchup. Grate the cheese.

NO CHIPOTLE?
If you can't find this smoky, hot chile paste, then use 1 tablespoon ketchup mixed with 1 teaspoon chile sauce and a pinch of smoked paprika, if you have it, instead. Add to the rest of the ingredients and adjust the seasoning with more sugar if you need to.

6

Return the peppers and onions to the pan, then stir in the chipotle sauce. Keep cooking until coated and sticky, then remove from the heat.

7

Warm the tortillas according to the package instructions. Spoon some of the chicken mixture onto each tortilla, sprinkle with cheese, then finish with sour cream and a few cilantro leaves. Roll up and eat immediately.

BURRITOS IN ADVANCE
Roll the tortillas with the chicken mixture only, then line them up in a large baking dish. Top with the cheese, then chill. When you're ready to eat, bake for 15 minutes at 400°F (200°C/Gas Mark 6) until melted, then top with the cilantro and sour cream.

Salmon with Dill Pickle & New Potatoes

Preparation time: 25 minutes
Cooking time: 5 minutes
Serves 4, easily halved

A classic combination that is quick and light enough for every day and ideal for weeknight entertaining too. The sour cream on the potatoes is a naughty-but-nice finish, or just toss them with the mustard and a little olive oil if you'd prefer. Trout fillets also work well and will take just a few minutes to cook.

1 lb 10 oz (750 g) new potatoes

1 cucumber

½ red onion

1 bunch fresh dill

2 tbsp white wine vinegar

1 tsp superfine (caster) sugar

4 salmon fillets, skin on

1 tsp olive oil, vegetable or
    sunflower oil

4 tbsp sour cream, crème fraîche or
    mayonnaise, half- or
    reduced-fat is fine

1 tsp whole-grain mustard

sea salt and freshly ground
    black pepper

1

Cut any larger potatoes in half, then put them into a pan of cold, salted water and bring to a boil. Cook for 15–20 minutes, until tender in the middle.

2

Meanwhile peel the cucumber, then remove the seeds using a teaspoon. Discard the seeds, then chop the flesh into small pieces.

3

Finely chop the onion and most of the dill, then mix with the cucumber in a bowl. Pour the vinegar over the top, sprinkle in the sugar and season with salt and pepper. Set aside while you prepare the salmon.

4

Heat the broiler (grill). Set the salmon on a lightly-oiled baking sheet, season all over with salt and pepper, then top the flesh side with a sprig or two of dill.

5

When the potatoes are ready, drain them and set aside to cool a little. Now put the salmon under the broiler and cook for 5 minutes or until the fish is firm and pale pink all over, and just cooked through in the middle. If you're not sure, poke a knife carefully down between the flakes in the middle of one of the fillets: if they pull apart easily, then the fish is ready. You don't need to turn the salmon as it cooks.

COOKING OILY FISH

If you're new to cooking fish, then something naturally oily such as salmon, mackerel or sardines is a great place to start. The slightly fattier flesh is less quick to dry out, and tends not to stick to the pan. Remember that just like a piece of meat, a fillet of fish will continue to cook as it sits on the plate, so it's always best to undercook rather than overcook it.

6

Stir the warm potatoes, cream or mayonnaise, and mustard together until coated, then season to taste with salt and pepper.

7

Lift the salmon onto plates, then top with a spoonful of the pickled cucumber and serve with the potatoes.

Easy Ciabatta Pizzas

Preparation time: 5 minutes
Cooking time: 10 minutes
Serves 2–4, easily doubled

This is more of a suggestion than a recipe really—if you don't have goat cheese or would rather use mozzarella, then fine. Ham instead of salami, mushrooms instead of tomatoes, red onions instead of olives… just use what you have to hand. No need to buy pizza-topping sauce either—just use tomato paste (purée) and dried herbs.

---

3 tbsp tomato paste (purée)

2 tsp dried oregano or mixed
    dried herbs

2 tbsp extra-virgin olive oil, plus
    extra for drizzling

1 fat clove garlic

1 large ciabatta loaf

1 x 4-oz (120-g) log of goat cheese

2–3 tomatoes

10 slices spicy salami or pepperoni

½ cup (50 g) black or green
    pitted olives

1 handful arugula (rocket) or fresh
    flat-leaf parsley

sea salt and freshly ground
    black pepper

salad, to serve (optional)

1

Mix the tomato paste (purée), most of the oregano, the olive oil, and some salt and pepper in a bowl. Crush the garlic and stir into the mixture.

2

Preheat the broiler (grill). Cut the bread in half lengthwise, then put onto a baking sheet, cut side up. Put under the broiler for 2 minutes or until pale golden. Spread the sauce over the bread, making sure that you go all the way to the edges.

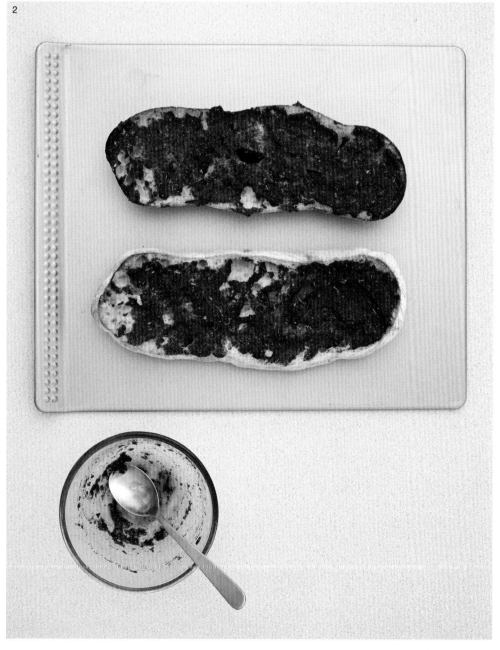

3

Slice or crumble the goat cheese and slice the tomatoes.

4

Arrange the cheese, tomatoes, salami and olives over the bread without overlapping too much—that way everything will get a good blast from the heat of the broiler. Try and cover the edges of the bread too, so that they don't singe. Sprinkle with a little more oregano and some black pepper, then drizzle with oil to help everything meld together.

5

Broil (grill) the pizzas for about 10 minutes, or until the cheese, tomatoes, and salami are starting to turn golden. Serve with a scattering of arugula (rocket) or parsley leaves and a fresh salad if you like.

3

4

Pasta Salad with Tomato Pesto

Preparation time: 10 minutes
Cooking time: 8 minutes
Serves 6 as part of a picnic

This salad has a big personality, with plenty of punch from the sun-dried or sun-blushed tomatoes, the latter of which will give a slightly looser pesto. The pesto makes twice as much as you need, so keep leftovers under a layer of oil for up to 2 weeks in the fridge.

3½ cups (400 g) small pasta shapes, such as macaroni
1¾ cups (100 g) sun-dried or sun-blushed tomatoes packed in oil
more extra-virgin olive oil, if needed
1 fat clove garlic
¾ cup (80 g) toasted pine nuts
1 bunch fresh basil
2 oz (50 g) Parmesan cheese
4½ oz (130 g) crimini (chestnut) mushrooms
5 oz (150 g) cherry tomatoes
3½ oz (100 g) baby spinach
1 lemon
sea salt and freshly ground black pepper

1

Bring a large pan of salted water to a boil, then add the pasta. Let the pan return to a boil, stirring once to prevent the pasta from sticking, then cook for 8 minutes, until the pasta is just tender. It's best to slightly undercook pasta if it's to be served in a salad, as it will absorb the dressing and can easily become too soggy.

2

For the pesto, drain the sun-dried tomatoes in a strainer (sieve) over a bowl. Put them into a food processor and add 2/3 cup (150 ml) of the oil. If there's not quite enough oil in the jar, add some of your own olive oil. Add the garlic, pine nuts and basil leaves.

TOASTING PINE NUTS
If you can't find pre-toasted pine nuts, then simply toast your own. Heat a skillet or frying pan over a low heat. Add the pine nuts and cook for about 3 minutes, stirring often, or until golden in places and smelling toasted.

3

Pulse the pesto ingredients together until almost smooth. Finely grate the Parmesan and add it to the bowl. Give it another quick pulse until the Parmesan and sauce are combined. Season with salt and pepper to taste.

4

Thinly slice the mushrooms, halve the cherry tomatoes and squeeze the juice from the lemon.

5

When the pasta is ready, reserve a cupful of the cooking water, then drain the pasta in a colander. Cool the pasta under cold running water, drain well, then toss with a little oil. The oil will prevent the pasta from sticking together.

6

Toss the pasta with half of the pesto, all of the lemon juice and, if it looks a little dry, some of the reserved cooking water.

7

Toss in the sliced mushrooms, tomatoes and spinach, then serve. If making the salad ahead, toss the mushrooms through but leave the spinach piled on top of the pasta—then mix when you're ready to eat.

Fattoush Salad with Labneh

Preparation time: 20 minutes,
plus standing
Cooking time: about 10 minutes
Serves 4–6 as part of a picnic

This is my version of fattoush,
a Lebanese salad which is usually
made with toasted pita bread.
I usually use tortillas, as they cook
to a delicious light crunch, but you
could try pita too. Labneh is a very
thick yogurt that goes really well
with the salad.

generous 2 cups (500 g) plain
   Greek yogurt
3 large or 4 smaller flour
   tortillas or wraps
2–3 uncooked beets (beetroot)
   (or you can use carrots)
½ head iceberg lettuce
1 bunch scallions (spring onions)
7 oz (200 g) cherry tomatoes
1 cucumber
1 bunch fresh flat-leaf parsley
1 clove garlic
1 lemon
3 tbsp extra-virgin olive oil
1 tsp honey
1 generous tsp dried mint
1 generous tsp sumac
sea salt and freshly ground
   black pepper

1
Preheat the oven to 350°F (180°C/ Gas Mark 4). Make the labneh first. Spoon the yogurt into a strainer (sieve) set over a bowl, cover with plastic wrap (clingfilm), then let stand in the fridge for 30 minutes, or longer if you can (overnight is ideal). This will cause the liquid part of the yogurt to drain away.

LABNEH
This is just another name for thickened yogurt, sometimes referred to as home-made soft cheese, as the yogurt takes on an intensely creamy and thick texture as the whey separates from the curds. You can serve labneh as a dip; just stir in your choice of chopped herbs, a little lemon juice and some olive oil.

2
Snip the tortillas into small pieces, then spread over a large baking sheet.

3
Toast the tortillas in the oven for 10–12 minutes until golden and very crisp. You may need to move them around halfway through to make sure they brown evenly. Cool completely then pack into a plastic food storage bag and seal the top. These can easily be made a day ahead, if you like.

4
Trim, then either shred or coarsely grate the beets (beetroot). It's best to wear rubber gloves while you do this, as the juice stains everything it touches. Put into a large transportable bowl.

5

Finely shred the lettuce and scallions (spring onions), then cut the tomatoes in half. Cut the cucumber in half, lengthwise, then scoop out the seeds with a teaspoon and slice the flesh into half-moons. Roughly chop the parsley leaves. Pile on top of the beets, then cover or seal the bowl and keep in the fridge until needed.

6

Make the dressing. Crush the garlic. Squeeze the lemon juice and mix it with the garlic, oil, honey, dried mint, sumac, and salt and pepper. Dip a little of the bread or lettuce into it and taste. Adjust the seasoning or sweetness if you need to. Just before setting off for the picnic, pour the dressing over the salad—it will sink into the beets so the greens won't get soggy.

WHAT'S SUMAC?
Sumac is a berry that is dried and then finely ground. It's used widely in Lebanese cooking, and adds an authentic sharp but earthy, lemony tang. A good alternative would be to add the zest of the lemon to the dressing as well as the juice, plus a little pinch of smoked or ordinary paprika.

7

Spoon the drained yogurt into a container and season with salt and pepper. Discard the liquid.

8

When you're ready to serve, sprinkle the toasted tortilla chips over the salad, then toss well. Serve the salad with a dollop of the labneh.

Gazpacho

Preparation time: 20 minutes,
plus chilling
Serves 4, easily doubled

This is possibly the most refreshing meal you could eat. I've added a little horseradish and Worcestershire sauce to this Spanish classic, bringing a little rounded heat and piquancy, but leave them out if you are a purist. Also, should you be tempted, try adding a naughty little nip of vodka to the mix.

1 slice day-old, good-quality bread

⅔ cup (150 ml) tomato juice

1 lb 5 oz (600 g) ripe tomatoes

½ cucumber, about 7 oz (200 g)

1 bunch scallions (spring onions)

1–2 cloves garlic, depending on
    your taste

5 roasted red bell peppers from
    a jar, drained, about 4 oz (120 g)

4 tbsp extra-virgin olive oil, plus
    extra to drizzle

1 tbsp sherry vinegar

½ tsp grated horseradish

1–2 tsp supertine (caster) sugar

a couple of dashes
    Worcestershire sauce

sea salt and freshly ground
    black pepper

1
Remove the crusts from the bread, then soak the bread in the tomato juice for a couple of minutes.

2
Cut the tomatoes into big wedges, and cut out the hard cores.

3

Peel and chop the cucumber into chunky pieces. Trim the scallions (spring onions). Thinly slice the white parts of 2 of the scallions and set aside (you'll use those to garnish the soup later), then roughly chop the rest. Peel the garlic. Put the vegetables, bell peppers and garlic into a blender or food processor, then add the bread and tomato juice.

4

Process the soup until it's as smooth as you can get it. Depending on the size of the machine, you may need to do this in 2 batches. Blend in the olive oil and vinegar, then add the horseradish, sugar and Worcestershire sauce to taste. Season, then chill the soup thoroughly—this will take a couple of hours.

CHILLING SOUP
Make sure that the soup is well chilled before putting it into a flask. Alternatively, you could freeze it in a plastic bottle (leaving plenty of room for it to expand) and pack into the picnic basket. The defrosting soup will chill the rest of your feast. Shake well before pouring.

5

When ready to serve, pour the soup into small glasses or cups. If you're at home, add an ice cube or two. The garnish is optional if picnicking, but if you want to go to the effort, take along a little jar of olive oil. Sprinkle the soup with the reserved scallion, a little black pepper and then drizzle with the oil.

Ham, Mustard, & Fava (Broad) Bean Tart

Preparation time: about 1 hour,
plus chilling
Cooking time: 35–40 minutes
Serves 8–10 as part of a picnic

There are a lot of steps here, but if you
are new to making pastry and want
to do it right, then here's how. You
can also use ready-made pastry and
follow the recipe from step 5.

1¾ cups (225 g) all-purpose
   (plain) flour
¼ tsp fine salt
7 tbsp (100 g) unsalted butter,
   very cold
4 eggs
1½ lb (675 g) fava (broad) beans,
   in their pods
1⅓ cups (300 g) crème fraîche or
   sour cream
1 tbsp whole-grain mustard
1 bunch scallions (spring onions)
4 oz (120 g) good-quality, thickly
   sliced ham
sea salt and freshly ground
   black pepper

1
To make the pastry, first put the flour and salt into a large bowl. Cut the butter into small cubes and add to the bowl. Separate 1 egg (see page 61), dropping the yolk into a small bowl. Add 2 tablespoons cold water and beat to combine.

2
Rub the butter into the flour using your fingertips, until the mixture looks like fine crumbs. If you have a food processor, then simply pulse for a few seconds until fine (this will give a good result). It's important that the butter stays cool so that it can incorporate into the flour without becoming pasty. If you can feel it getting sticky, put the bowl into the fridge for a few minutes before you continue.

3
Drizzle the egg mixture evenly over the bowl, then work into a dough using a round-bladed knife. If you have a food processor, then add the egg and pulse it in gradually.

4
Place the dough onto the work surface and knead it briefly until smooth. (Or pulse the processor blades until the dough comes together in a smooth ball.) Shape into a flat disc, wrap in plastic wrap (clingfilm), then chill for 30 minutes.

5

While the pastry chills, prepare the fava (broad) beans. Bring a pan of salted water to a boil. While it comes to a boil, break the bean pods and take the beans out.

6

Boil the beans for 2 minutes. Drain in a strainer (sieve), then cool under cold running water to stop them cooking. Remove the bright green beans from their pale green jackets. This can take some time, so ask for a helping hand if there is one. The skins are a bit tough, so it's best to remove them unless your fava beans are very young and tender.

OUT OF SEASON?
If fresh fava beans aren't available, use 13 oz (375 g) frozen fava beans or even substitute with 6 oz (175 g) frozen petite peas (petit pois). The weight is less, as peas don't need to be double-podded.

7

To make the filling, put the remaining eggs into a large bowl and add the crème fraîche and mustard. Whisk together until smooth. Season with pepper and a little salt, then chill until needed. Chop the scallions (spring onions) and cut the ham into small pieces.

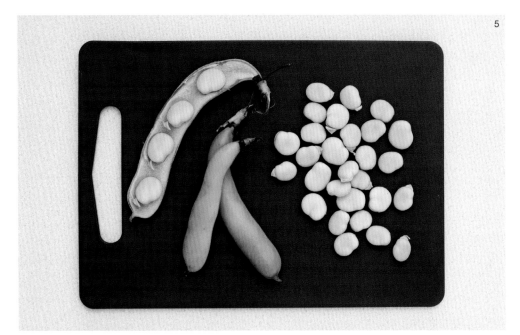

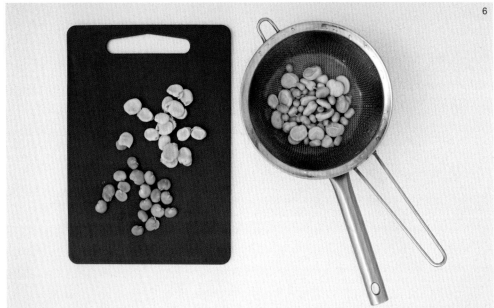

8

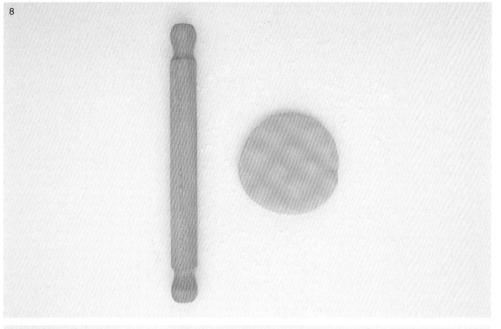

Dust the work surface and a rolling pin with flour. Have ready a 9-inch (23-cm) round, loose-bottom fluted tart pan. Using the rolling pin, press shallow ridges evenly across the pastry, then rotate it by a quarter turn. Repeat this until the pastry is about ½-inch (1-cm) thick. This will help the pastry to stretch without it becoming tough.

9

Now roll out the pastry. Push the rolling pin back and forth in one direction only, turning the pastry by a quarter turn every few rolls, until it's about ⅛-inch (4-mm) thick. Then, using the rolling pin to help, lift the pastry over the pan.

10

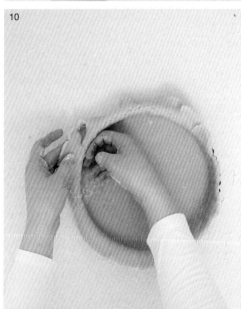

Ease the pastry gently into the pan, then press it gently into the fluted edge, using your knuckles and fingertips.

11

Roll the rolling pin over the pan, to remove the excess, then prick the base several times with a fork. Now gently press the pastry all around the sides of the pan, so that it rises about ⅛ inch (4 mm) above the rim. By doing this, your pastry will still come to the top of the pan once it's baked, even if it shrinks a little. Lift onto a baking sheet, then chill in the fridge for 20 minutes, until firm. Preheat the oven to 400°F (200°C/Gas Mark 6).

12

Tear a sheet of parchment paper large enough to completely cover the pan. Scrunch up the paper, then use it to line the pastry. Cover the paper with a layer of pie weights (baking beans), mounding them up a little at the edges, then bake for 20 minutes, still on the baking sheet, until the pastry is dry and pale.

PIE WEIGHTS
These ceramic balls are used to weigh pastry down as it cooks, keep it in place and prevent it from slipping down the edges of the pan. You can also use dried beans instead. Re-use them for baking only.

13

Remove the pie weights and paper, then bake the pastry for another 10 minutes, until pale golden and sandy to the touch all over. Turn the oven down to 325°F (160°C/Gas Mark 3).

14

Scatter the ham and fava beans over the pastry. To avoid spills, pull out the oven rack part-way, place the tart (on its sheet) on the rack, then pour in the egg mixture. Carefully slide the rack back in.

15

Bake the tart for 30–40 minutes, until the filling is set, with just the slightest wobble in the center. Cool on a rack, then chill until needed.

Tomato Pissaladière Tarts

Preparation time: 45 minutes
Cooking time: 15–20 minutes
Makes 6

With melting soft and sweet onions, tart tomatoes and salty anchovies and olives, these little lovelies bring a vibrant taste of Provence to your picnic basket. Bake on the morning of the picnic, cool completely, then stack up interleaved with parchment paper before packing.

---

3 large onions

2 tbsp extra-virgin olive oil, plus extra for drizzling

a few sprigs fresh thyme

1 lb 2 oz (500 g) ready-made puff pastry

a little all-purpose (plain) flour, for rolling out

3–4 ripe tomatoes

6 anchovy fillets in olive oil

scant 1 cup (100 g) black pitted olives

sea salt and freshly ground black pepper

1

3

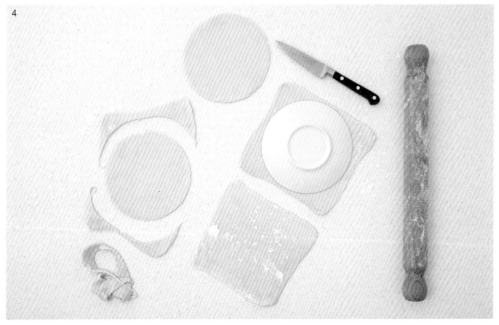

4

WHAT'S A PISSALADIÈRE?
Pissaladière is the French equivalent of pizza, normally made with a bread base, but in this case using crisp puff pastry.

1
Halve, then thinly slice the onions. Heat the oil in a large skillet or frying pan, then add the onions, and stir to coat. Season with salt and pepper, then strip the leaves from most of the thyme and add to the pan.

2
Cover the pan with a lid and cook the onions for 30 minutes, stirring now and then, until completely soft.

3
Take the lid off, then cook for another 5 minutes or so, turning the heat a little higher, until the onions are pale golden. Set aside to cool. These onions will keep perfectly happily in the fridge for a few days, if you want to get ahead.

4
While you wait for the onions to cook, prepare the pastry and other toppings. Cut the pastry into 6 equal pieces, and then, using a little flour, roll out each piece until it's about ⅛-inch (4-mm) thick. Using a small saucer or plate, cut each piece into a round.

5

Score a circle about ¾ inch (2 cm) in from the edge of the pastry. This will help the edges of the pastry to puff up around the filling later on. Put the circles onto 2 baking sheets lined with parchment paper, then chill for at least 10 minutes.

6

Thinly slice the tomatoes (you'll need three pieces per tart), then cut the anchovies in half lengthwise.

7

Spoon the onions onto the pastry, spreading them out evenly within the scored border (or thereabouts—you don't have to be too neat). Top with overlapping slices of tomato. Add the olives, then criss-cross the anchovies over the top. Sprinkle with the remaining thyme leaves and some pepper. You won't need salt, as the anchovies and olives will be salty enough. Drizzle with a little more oil.

8

Bake the tarts for 15–20 minutes, until the pastry is golden and puffed around the edges. Drizzle with a little more oil if you like. Serve the tarts warm or cold.

Spicy Chicken with Mango Raita

Preparation time: 20 minutes,
plus marinating
Cooking time: 40 minutes
Serves 6 as part of a picnic

You'll certainly keep meat-eaters happy with this picnic and summer party classic. The marinade, made with yogurt, tenderizes the chicken and cooks to a satisfying golden coating. Chicken must be thoroughly cooked and kept well-chilled to be food-safe. See page 20.

8 chicken pieces, drumsticks and
    thighs are best
2 tbsp cumin seeds
4 cloves garlic
1 tsp freshly ground black pepper
1 tsp chili flakes (or 2 dried
    chiles, crushed)
1 tbsp olive oil
1¼ cups (300 g) plain yogurt
2 limes
1 large bunch fresh cilantro
    (coriander)
1 large ripe mango
1 bunch scallions (spring onions)
sea salt and freshly ground
    black pepper

1

First pull the skin from the chicken. The easiest way to remove it from the drumsticks is to grip the skin with a piece of paper towel and pull (as if you are removing socks). Now slash each piece of chicken 2–3 times, right down to the bone.

2

Using a mortar and pestle, lightly crush the cumin seeds to release their aroma. Crush the garlic. Put both into a mixing bowl then add the pepper, chili flakes, olive oil, and 3 tablespoons of the yogurt. Squeeze the juice from 1 lime and add to the bowl. Finely chop the cilantro (coriander) and add half to the bowl.

3

Mix the ingredients well, then add the chicken, and toss to coat with your hands, making sure plenty of the marinade is pushed into the slashes in the meat. Cover and let marinate in the fridge for at least 30 minutes and up to 24 hours.

4

To make the raita, cut off segments of the mango as close to the pit (stone) as you can. Then cut away any flesh from around the middle. Cut deep criss-crossed cuts into the mango, stopping when you get to the skin, then push the flesh inside out so it looks like a hedgehog. Cut away the flesh.

CHOOSING MANGOS
A ripe mango will smell fragrant and yield slightly when pressed. All mangos start off green but will ripen to anything from a gentle yellow to vibrant pink and orange, depending on the variety. Once ripe, keep in the fridge. Alfonso mangos are revered for their sweet flesh. If you are lucky enough to find some, use two in this recipe, as they are smaller than regular mangos.

5

Chop the mango, thinly slice the scallions (spring onions), then mix with the remaining yogurt. Add a squeeze of juice from half of the second lime, the rest of the chopped cilantro and season to taste. Pack into a lidded container and keep chilled.

6

When ready to cook the chicken, preheat the oven to 375°F (190°C/ Gas Mark 5). Put the chicken into a roasting pan and roast for 40 minutes, turning halfway through cooking, until golden and crusty. The marinade can stick to the pan, so line with aluminum foil if you want, to save on the clean-up later.

7

Let the chicken cool completely, then pack into a lidded container with the rest of the lime, cut into wedges. Keep cool. When you get to the picnic, serve with the raita and squeeze the lime over the meat.

Pans Bagnats

Preparation time: 15 minutes,
plus 2 hours standing
Cooking time: 7 minutes
Makes 6

Pans bagnats are a typical Provençal
lunchtime bite. Essentially a salad
niçoise sandwich, these hearty stuffed
loaves are ideal for picnics, as the
ingredients need a couple of hours
to mingle and improve. If someone in
the party doesn't like fish, then slice
some good salami and add that to
their sandwich instead of the tuna.

4 eggs
6 individual baguettes or mini
    ciabatta loaves
1 clove garlic
2 tbsp red wine vinegar
8 oz (225 g) good-quality tuna
    packed in olive oil
6 ripe tomatoes
6 roasted red bell peppers from
    a jar, drained (I used Spanish
    piquillo peppers)
4 tbsp dry black pitted
    olives (or you could use a
    spoonful of tapenade)
1 generous tbsp capers in
    brine, drained
1 handful fresh basil
sea salt and freshly ground
    black pepper

1
Put the eggs into a pan of cold water and set over high heat, then bring to a boil. Start a kitchen timer when big bubbles start to rise every few seconds. Boil the eggs for 7 minutes for yolks that are firm, but not totally dry in the middle.

2
While you wait, scoop out the crumb from the insides of the baguettes or loaves—this will give room for the filling. You could use this for the gazpacho on page 114 or save it for bread crumbs. Cool the eggs under a couple of changes of cold water.

3

Crush the garlic, mix with the vinegar and 3 tablespoons oil from the tuna, then season with salt and pepper. Drizzle some dressing over the insides of the bread, to moisten.

4

Slice the tomatoes and eggs. Layer up the tomatoes, bell peppers, olives, capers, egg, basil leaves and tuna in the bread, seasoning and adding a little of the dressing as you go. Tear the peppers with your fingers if you need to.

5

Sandwich the baguettes or rolls back together, then wrap each one in parchment paper and tie with two pieces of string. Let stand for 2 hours at room temperature before cutting in half to eat. If you'd like to make these further ahead of time, chill, then take out of the fridge 2 hours before the picnic, although the bread might not stay as crusty.

Spinach Ricotta Pastries with Sweet Bell Pepper Dip

Preparation time: 30 minutes,
plus cooling
Cooking time: 20 minutes
Makes about 18 pastries

Bring these pastries along to your picnic as a delicious veggie-friendly option. I especially like to use Spanish piquillo peppers for the dip, which have a deep smoky edge to them and a deep, vibrant red color.

---

14 oz (400 g) baby spinach
9 oz (250 g) crimini (chestnut)
   mushrooms
2 tbsp extra-virgin olive oil
6 tbsp (80 g) unsalted butter
whole nutmeg, for grating
9 oz (250 g) ricotta cheese, drained
   of any liquid
1 egg
12 large sheets filo pastry, thawed
   if frozen
1 jar roasted red bell peppers,
   6 oz (175 g) drained weight
1 clove garlic
sea salt and freshly ground
   black pepper

1
Bring a full kettle of water to a boil. Put the spinach into a colander.

2
Pour the just-boiled water slowly and evenly over the spinach, until it has wilted right down. Cool the spinach under cold running water, then squeeze out all the water you can using your hands (or you can put it in a clean dish towel and wring it dry).

3
Slice the mushrooms. Heat 1 tablespoon of oil and 1 teaspoon of the butter in a skillet or frying pan. When the butter foams, add the mushrooms and fry for 5 minutes, or until golden and the pan is dry.

4
Add the spinach to the pan with the mushrooms and cook for a couple of minutes to evaporate any remaining liquid (this will keep the pastries crisp later). Season with plenty of salt and pepper, and about ¼ teaspoon finely grated nutmeg. Tip into a bowl and cool.

5
When the vegetables are cold or nearly cold, add the ricotta, break in the egg, and mix well to combine. Season to taste with salt and pepper. The filling can be made and chilled a day ahead, if you like.

6

Preheat the oven to 400°F (200°C/Gas Mark 6). Melt the remaining butter in a small pan. Unwrap the pastry, take out 2 sheets, then cover the rest with plastic wrap (clingfilm) or a dish towel to prevent it from drying out. With the long edge facing you, cut the pastry into three equal strips. The pastry used in the photos was 9½ × 11 inches (24 × 28 cm), but different brands vary, so adjust as necessary. Brush the top pieces with melted butter.

7

Spoon a generous tablespoon of the filling onto the bottom of one of the strips, then fold the corner over to make a triangle shape. Keep folding the triangle over and over until you have made a neat little pastry. Brush the outside with a little butter, then set on a baking sheet. The pastries can be chilled at this point and baked next day, if you like.

8

To make the dip, put the bell peppers, peeled garlic and remaining oil into a pitcher (jug) and process until smooth using an immersion (stick) blender. You could use a food processor instead, or just chop the peppers very finely and mix with the crushed garlic and oil. Season to taste.

9

On the day of the picnic, bake the pasties for 20 minutes, or until crisp, puffed, and golden. Let cool; then pack into your picnic box. Serve with the bell pepper dip.

Cobb Salad with Honey Mustard Dressing

Preparation time: 20 minutes
Serves 4–6 as part of a picnic

This useful salad will accommodate more or less anything you put in it, plus there's no danger of it getting soggy. Just make sure that you layer the ingredients in a sensible order—heavier things at the bottom, delicate at the top, and keep the buttermilk dressing separate until the final moment.

8 strips (rashers) smoked bacon
   (dry-cured is best)
3–4 eggs
1 x 2¼-lb (1-kg) cooked chicken
2 ripe avocados
2 tsp red or white wine vinegar
1 head Romaine lettuce
²/₃ cup (150 ml) buttermilk or low-fat
   plain yogurt
1 small clove garlic
1 tbsp honey
1 tbsp whole-grain mustard
1 handful fresh chives, or you could
   use scallions (spring onions)
   if you have some
sea salt and freshly ground
   black pepper

1

Heat a nonstick skillet or frying pan over a medium heat. Snip or cut the bacon into bite-size pieces, then add to the pan. Fry over medium heat for 5 minutes, or until crisp and the fat has run out of the meat. Set the bacon aside on paper towels, letting the excess fat drain away.

2

Meanwhile, put the eggs into a pan of cold water, then bring to a boil. Start a kitchen timer when big bubbles start to rise every few seconds. Boil the eggs for 7 minutes for yolks that are firm, but not totally dry in the middle.

3

Cool the eggs under a couple of changes of cold water, then peel and cut into quarters.

4

Tear the chicken into bite-size pieces, discarding the skin and the bones. Put into the bottom of a large transportable bowl or container. It's easier to tear the meat from a warm chicken than cold. If using just-cooked chicken, make sure that you let the meat cool completely before putting it into the picnic bowl (see tips on page 11 if you need more information on food safety).

5

Cut the avocado in half, then remove the pit (stone). Slice criss-crossed lines in the flesh, cutting down to, but not through, the skin. Scoop out the pieces of avocado with a spoon and drop into a bowl. Toss with 1 teaspoon of the vinegar to prevent the flesh from turning brown.

6

Shred the lettuce and use it to cover the chicken. Romaine is robust, but if you are using a delicate leaf, such as arugula (rocket), save it for the top of the salad. Top with the avocado, then the bacon and eggs, and sprinkle with a little salt and pepper. Seal the container and keep in the fridge. The salad can be assembled up to a day ahead.

7

Put the buttermilk or yogurt into a jar. Crush the garlic, add to the jar with the remaining vinegar, the honey, and mustard, plus some salt and pepper. Snip in the chives using kitchen shears (scissors). Seal the jar and shake to combine.

8

When you get to the picnic, dig into the bowl to make sure everyone gets a bit of everything, give the dressing a quick shake, then drizzle over each serving.

FOOD FOR FRIENDS

Herb-Crusted Lamb with Pea Puree & Tomatoes

Preparation time: 20 minutes,
plus resting
Cooking time: 20 minutes
Serves 6

Depending on your guests' appetites,
serve two or three cutlets per person.
Fully trimmed lamb (shown right) is
also known as "French trimmed". All
of the skin, fat and meat from around
the main eye of meat and the bones
are removed, to give a very neat
effect that looks special on the plate,
and is easy to carve and eat.

1 handful fresh thyme

1½ cups (80 g) fresh bread crumbs

2 tbsp extra-virgin olive oil, plus
    extra for drizzling

2 racks of lamb, with 7– 8 cutlets
    each, fully trimmed (ask your
    butcher to do this for you)

1 generous tbsp Dijon mustard

1 large or 2 small onions

6 tbsp (80 g) unsalted butter

3½ cups (400 g) frozen peas or
    shelled fresh peas

scant 1 cup (200 ml) vegetable
    broth (stock)

6 small bunches cherry tomatoes

1 handful fresh mint

sea salt and freshly ground
    black pepper

1
Pick the leaves from the thyme (you'll need about 2 tablespoons), finely chop, then mix with the bread crumbs, oil, and some salt and pepper. This can be made up to a day ahead, if you like.

2
Cut the racks of lamb into portions of 3 or 4 cutlets each. Season with salt and pepper, then smear the mustard over the top of each rack.

3
Press the bread crumb mixture onto the racks using the palm of your hand. The racks can now be chilled for up to a day. Remember to remove them from the fridge 1 hour before cooking, so that your meat cooking times correspond with mine.

4
For the pea puree, roughly chop the onion. Melt the butter in a medium pan, then add the onion with some salt and pepper. Cook gently for 10 minutes, until very soft.

5

Add the peas and broth (stock) to the pan. Bring to a boil, then simmer for 2 minutes, or until the peas are bright and tender.

6

Using an immersion (stick) blender, blend the peas until thick and smooth, then season to taste with salt and pepper. If you don't have a blender, you can puree the peas in a blender or food processor or push through a strainer instead.

7

Preheat the oven to 400°F (200°C/ Gas Mark 6). Roast the lamb for 20 minutes, adding the tomatoes to the pan halfway through cooking. When the lamb is ready, the crumbs will be golden and the tomatoes starting to split and turn juicy. These timings will cook the lamb medium rare: pink and juicy in the middle. If you like meat well done, add an extra 5 minutes (although this will make the meat tougher and drier and I wouldn't recommend it).

8

Let the lamb rest in the roasting pan for 5 minutes, then slice it into cutlets (you could serve the racks whole if you like, but carving makes it easier for your guests to eat).

9

Spoon the pea puree onto plates, top with the lamb, then finish with a bunch of tomatoes, a drizzle of olive oil, and a scattering of torn mint leaves.

Roast Chicken with Tarragon Sauce

Preparation time: 10 minutes
Cooking time: 1 hour 20 minutes
Serves 4–6

Ideal for a spring Sunday, this chicken will have everyone asking for more (and it's all cooked in one pan, too). Tarragon, classic with chicken and creamy dishes, can be replaced with flat-leaf parsley or chervil. Cook two chickens together if your family has a big appetite.

---

1 x 3¼-lb (1.5-kg) chicken

1 onion

1 lemon

1 handful fresh tarragon

1 tbsp unsalted butter

1 lb 10 oz (750 g) small new potatoes

1 tbsp olive oil

9 oz (250 g) asparagus or green beans

scant ½ cup (100 ml) dry white wine

⅔ cup (150 ml) heavy (double) cream

1¼ cups (300 ml) chicken broth (stock)

5 oz (150 g) frozen peas

sea salt and freshly ground
   black pepper

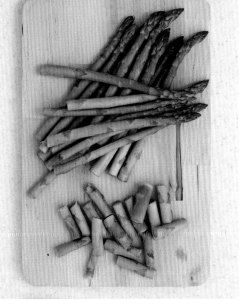

1

Preheat the oven to 400°F (200°C/ Gas Mark 6). Put the chicken on a board, then snip away any string that had been used to truss the bird. Remove the giblets from the cavity (the gap between the legs). Cut the onion and lemon in half, then put half the onion, half the lemon, and a small bunch of tarragon into the cavity.

2

Loosely retie the legs together with string. Spread the butter over the breast and thigh meat, then season with plenty of salt and pepper. Place the chicken in a roasting pan and roast for 20 minutes.

TRUSSING POULTRY

When chickens and turkeys are trussed too tightly, it makes it more difficult for the heat to permeate through the body. This means that the breast meat, which doesn't need so much cooking, can overcook while you wait for the inner meat of the thigh to cook completely. Tying more loosely means that the hot air can circulate all around the meat.

3

Cut any larger potatoes in half, then add to the pan once the chicken has roasted for 20 minutes. Drizzle with 1 tablespoon oil and toss with any juices in the bottom of the pan. Return to the oven for another 40 minutes.

4

Cut the bottom 2 inches (5 cm) from each asparagus spear, as the ends can often be a bit tough. Cut the asparagus into finger-length pieces.

5

When the chicken is golden and cooked, and the potatoes are tender, transfer everything to a large plate. Put into the (turned off) oven, leaving the door ajar, to keep the chicken warm as it rests.

TESTING WHETHER A WHOLE CHICKEN IS COOKED
Your chicken is ready if the legs wobble freely at the hip joints—this indicates that the meat has cooked and contracted in the thickest part of the bird, making the legs loose. Another way to test is to insert a skewer into the thickest part of the thigh. If the juices come out clear or with no trace of pink, the bird is cooked.

6

While the chicken rests, it's time to make the sauce and cook the green vegetables. Spoon away the excess fat from the roasting pan. Heat the pan over low heat, then add the wine and bubble for 1 minute. Add the cream and broth (stock).

7

Add the asparagus to the pan, then simmer for 3 minutes. Add the peas, then return to a boil until the vegetables are just tender.

8

Roughly chop the rest of the tarragon and stir it into the sauce. Season the sauce to taste—add a splash of the juice from the remaining lemon half if you like. Serve the chicken with the potatoes and the creamy vegetables.

Seared Tuna with Sauce Vierge

Preparation time: 15 minutes
Cooking time: less than 5 minutes
Serves 4–6

Sauce vierge, meaning "virgin sauce," is a classic partner for fish. Once you've mastered this recipe, try it with salmon or white fish. It's really important that you choose tuna carefully, as some stocks are under great pressure and not fished in a sustainable way. Avoid bluefin tuna and ask your fish supplier for sustainable alternatives.

---

1 lb 10 oz (750 g) new potatoes

1 shallot

2 tbsp white wine vinegar

9 oz (250 g) cherry tomatoes

1 handful fresh tarragon

1 handful fresh chives

1 tbsp small capers in brine, drained

6 tbsp extra-virgin olive oil, plus
    extra for drizzling

11 oz (300 g) fine green beans

1 tbsp unsalted butter

4 or 6 thick, sustainably sourced
    tuna steaks (or any other
    firm-fleshed fish)

1 tsp ground coriander

sea salt and freshly ground
    black pepper

1

Thickly slice the potatoes, put into a large pan of salted cold water, then bring to a boil and cook for 7 minutes, or until they start to soften around the edges. Start making the sauce vierge while you wait. Finely chop the shallot, put it into a bowl, and pour the vinegar over it. It will start to soften and sweeten up the shallot a little.

2

Cut the tomatoes into quarters. Finely chop the tarragon and chives. Add these to the shallot bowl with the capers and olive oil, then season to taste with salt and pepper.

3

Trim the stem ends from the beans, then add to the pan with the potatoes. Let it come back to a boil, then cook for 4–5 minutes, until both the potatoes and beans are tender.

4

Drain the potatoes and beans, return to the hot pan, then toss with the butter and set aside. The vegetables should be warm, not hot, in the final dish, which gives you time to concentrate on the fish.

5

When you're ready to serve, heat a grill pan (griddle), skillet or frying pan. Pat the fish dry with paper towels, then put it onto a plate. Sprinkle on both sides with the coriander and some salt and pepper.

6

When the pan is very hot but not smoking, drizzle the fish with a little oil, then add it to the pan. Cook for 2 minutes on each side, which will leave it slightly pink in the middle. Don't try to move the fish as it cooks, as it needs time to make a golden crust, which will help it to release easily from the pan. As soon as the tuna is cooked, take it out of the pan, as it can overcook very quickly.

COOKING FOR LARGE GROUPS
If you want to cook this for more than 6 people, you'll probably need to cook the fish in 2 batches, unless you have a very large pan. Slightly undercook the first batch, then put it into a very low oven while you cook the second. Keep the heat high and avoid overcrowding the pan to get the best result.

7

Spoon the warm vegetables onto serving plates, then top with the tuna. Spoon the dressing over the fish and serve.

Steak & Artichoke Tagliata

Preparation time: 10 minutes,
plus marinating and resting
Cook time: 5 minutes
Serves 2, easily doubled or more

Italians love to eat tagliata (which translates as "cut"), a classic combination of char-grilled steak, peppery leaves and shaved Parmesan. I think it's the perfect alternative to good old steak and fries (chips) when the weather heats up. The steak in the photographs is sirloin, but you can choose from other cuts too (see page 160).

1 x 9-oz (250-g) filet, sirloin or rump
   steak, trimmed of excess fat
2 sprigs fresh rosemary
1 tbsp extra-virgin olive oil, plus
   1 tsp (you can use the oil from
   the artichokes, if they're packed
   in extra-virgin)
2 oz (50 g) wild arugula (rocket)
3 oz (80 g) char-grilled artichoke
   hearts preserved in oil, drained
small chunk of Parmesan cheese,
   for shaving
2 tsp small capers in brine, drained
2 tsp balsamic vinegar
sea salt and freshly ground
   black pepper

1

3

1

Put the steak onto a plate. Finely chop the rosemary needles, then rub them all over the steak with 1 teaspoon oil. Cover and let marinate for at least 30 minutes at room temperature, or up to 24 hours in the fridge.

STEAK TEMPERATURE
Very cold meat is more likely to overcook, as it takes longer for heat to reach the center. Either marinate the steak ahead of time, then remove from the fridge 30 minutes before cooking, or take the steak from the fridge, rub with the marinade and set aside for at least 30 minutes.

2

Heat a grill pan (griddle) until very hot. Season the steak generously. Add the steak to the pan, then let it cook, without moving it, for 2 minutes (or 2½ minutes if it's particularly thick). Press the steak a few times with your tongs or a spatula to encourage a deep, golden crust underneath.

GRIDDLING MEAT
It's better to oil the meat than to add oil to the pan—this will reduce the amount of smoke that will come from the pan. If the steak doesn't make a loud sizzle as soon as it hits the pan, then the pan isn't hot enough—take the steak out. Keeping the heat high encourages the meat to develop a brown crust and good flavor.

3

After 2 minutes, turn the steak over and cook for 2 minutes more. If the steak has fat around the edge, hold it fat-edge down against the pan and cook for about 30 seconds, until golden.

4

Transfer the steak to a plate, cover loosely and let rest for 2 minutes, or until surrounded with juices.

WHICH STEAK?
It's up to you what kind of steak you choose: filet is the most tender, but also the costliest cut. As filet has little fat throughout the meat, it's best cooked on the rarer side. Sirloin is a good all-round choice, with a fair marbling of fat but still very tender. Rump is a tasty, good-value cut, but can be less tender than sirloin.

5

While the steak rests, scatter the arugula (rocket) and artichokes over a platter. Use a vegetable peeler to shave the Parmesan, or just grate it coarsely. You'll need a small handful.

6

Using a sharp knife, cut the steak into thick slices.

7

Nestle the steak into the salad, then pour the resting juices over it. Sprinkle the salad with the Parmesan, capers, then the oil and vinegar. Serve immediately.

Crisp Duck & Pineapple Salad

Preparation time: 20 minutes,
plus marinating time
Cooking time: about 15 minutes
Serves 2, easily doubled or more

I often serve this for supper, as it's
refreshing, vibrant and lighter than
a Thai curry. I like to use duck, but
the salad is also really good with
pork tenderloin, thinly sliced steak,
or even shrimp (prawns). Serve
with simply cooked rice, if you need
something more substantial.

---

2 plump duck breasts, skin on

2 tsp Chinese five-spice, or
   Thai seven-spice powder

5 tbsp plus 1 tsp vegetable oil

3 shallots

1 tbsp all-purpose (plain) flour

1 fennel bulb

1 small, ripe pineapple, about
   2 lb (900 g) total weight

1 small clove garlic

3 tbsp roasted peanuts

1 tbsp light brown (muscovado)
   sugar

1 fat red chile

1 lime

1 tbsp fish sauce

1 bunch Thai or ordinary basil

sea salt and freshly ground
   black pepper

1

Score criss-cross lines into the duck skin using a very sharp knife. Take care not to cut down into the flesh. Scoring the skin like this will help the duck to cook evenly without shrinking and to release the fat from the skin as it cooks.

2

Put the duck onto a plate, then sprinkle with the spice powder and 1 teaspoon of the oil. Rub the spices right into the meat and skin. If you have time, cover with plastic wrap (clingfilm) and let the duck marinate in the fridge for a few hours. Take it out of the fridge 30 minutes before you want to cook it. If not, then the time it takes you to make the salad will suffice.

3

Thinly slice the shallots and toss them in the flour with a pinch of salt. Heat the oil in a pan for a few minutes. Line a plate or bowl with a few sheets of paper towel, ready for draining in a few minutes' time.

PEELING SHALLOTS
If you find the skins won't come away from the shallots easily, then try this simple trick. Cover the shallots with boiling water, then let soak for 5 minutes. Drain, then peel.

4

Shake the excess flour from half the shallots, then pan-fry for 3–4 minutes, until golden brown all over and very crisp. You'll need to stir them around to make sure they brown evenly, and take care toward the end of cooking, as they can easily burn. When the shallots are ready, use a slotted spoon to lift them from the oil and onto the paper to drain. Repeat with the second batch.

5

Cut the fennel bulb in half and remove any very tough outer layers. Thinly slice the fennel. Reserve the feathery leaves, if there are any.

6

Cut away the top and bottom of the pineapple, then cut away the spiky brown skin, removing all traces of brown from the flesh. A serrated knife is best for this job. Cut the pineapple into quarters, cut out the central paler and tougher core, then thinly slice the flesh. Add to the bowl with the fennel.

IS MY PINEAPPLE RIPE?
To check that your pineapple is ripe and ready to use, tug gently on one of the inner leaves sprouting from the crown. If it comes away easily, then it's ready to eat. The fruit should also have an enticing sweet and fragrant smell.

7
To make the dressing, put the garlic, peanuts, and sugar into a mortar. Very roughly chop half of the chile, including the seeds, and add that too.

8
Pound the ingredients with a pestle to make a very rough paste. Squeeze the juice from the lime. Mix in the fish sauce and 2 tablespoons of the lime juice and set aside. Dip a little bit of fennel into the dressing and check for seasoning. Add more sugar, chile, lime, or fish sauce if you think it needs it, but remember that the pineapple will add lots of tang later on.

NO MORTAR AND PESTLE?
If you don't have a mortar and pestle, then you can pulse everything together in a small food processor, or simply crush the garlic, finely chop the chile and peanuts, then mix with the other ingredients.

9
When you're ready to eat, season the duck breasts with salt and pepper, then put them skin-side down into a cold skillet or frying pan. Heat the pan over medium heat, then wait until the fat starts to run from the skin and you can hear a sizzle. Cook the duck for 8 minutes on this side, until most of the fat has run out from under the skin and the skin is crisp and golden. Spoon away most of the excess fat. Turn the duck over, then cook for another 6 minutes. This will give you duck that is just pink and juicy in the middle.

10

Set the duck on a board, then let it rest for 2–3 minutes. Slice the meat diagonally with a large knife.

RESTING MEAT
It's really important to let meat rest before you slice it. A couple of minutes will be enough for small pieces of meat or poultry like this—you want it to relax, but not to get cold. Cooking meat at high temperatures causes the muscle fibers to contract. As the meat rests, they loosen again. A rested piece of meat will be sitting in a little pool of juice and be easier to carve and tender to eat.

11

Toss the peanut dressing with the fennel and pineapple, then tear in the basil leaves.

12

Scoop the salad onto serving plates, then top with the duck, sprinkle with the crispy shallots and serve with more sliced red chiles if you like.

Lemon & Basil Gnudi

Preparation time: 30 minutes,
plus at least 1 hour chilling
Cooking time: 15 minutes
Serves 4–6 (makes a great starter
too)

Cousins to potato gnocchi, gnudi
are little ricotta dumplings, which are
are lighter, simpler to make, and
a fantastic option for a vegetarian
who's seen it all at dinner parties.
If fresh fava (broad) beans are
unavailable, boil 1 lb 2 oz (500 g)
frozen beans instead, and then
remove their pale green skins.

2¼ cups (500 g) ricotta cheese,
    drained of any liquid
1 egg
1 bunch fresh basil
1 organic (unwaxed) lemon
4 oz (120 g) Parmesan cheese
1 tbsp all-purpose (plain) flour, plus
    plenty more for shaping
½ cup (25 g) fresh white
    bread crumbs
2¼ lb (1 kg) fresh fava (broad) beans
2 cloves garlic
6 tbsp (80 g) butter
1 tsp dried chili flakes
sea salt and freshly ground
    black pepper

1

Put the ricotta and egg into a large mixing bowl. Roughly chop half the basil leaves, add to the mixture, then finely grate in the zest of the lemon and three-quarters of the Parmesan. Season with plenty of pepper and a little salt. Reserve the lemon.

2

Beat the ingredients together until smooth, then sift in the flour and add the bread crumbs.

3

Stir the flour and bread crumbs into the ricotta mixture. Put plenty of flour in a large baking pan or something similar, and have a floured plate ready. Spoon a couple of generous teaspoons of the gnudi mixture separately into the flour in the pan, then roll them around in the flour until well coated. Shape the gnudi with dry hands to make a smooth ball or oval. Put onto the floured plate, then repeat with the rest of the mixture. Chill the gnudi for at least 1 hour, or up to 24 hours. This will firm up the gnudi and make them ready for cooking.

4

Prepare the fava (broad) beans. Bring a pan of salted water to a boil. While it comes to a boil, break the pods and pop the beans out. Discard the pods.

5

Boil the beans for 3 minutes, by which point they should have floated to the top of the pan. Drain in a strainer (sieve) and cool under cold running water, then remove the bright green beans from their pale green skins. Cool under cold running water and set aside for later.

6

When you're ready to cook the gnudi, bring a large, deep pan of well-salted water to a boil and put some serving plates in a low oven to warm. Add half of the gnudi to the pan (drop them in carefully, one at a time, and they won't stick). They will rise up to the surface. Once this has happened, cook for another 2–3 minutes, then lift out and onto the warmed plates. Repeat until all of the gnudi are cooked. When ready, the gnudi will feel firm and bounce back when pressed lightly.

7

Just before serving, prepare the buttery sauce. Crush the garlic. Heat a skillet or frying pan over medium-high heat, add the butter and let it melt. Add the garlic and chili flakes, then sizzle for 1 minute.

8

Add the shelled fava beans and remaining basil leaves and splash in a good squeeze of juice from the lemon—the butter will sizzle a little here and turn slightly golden. Season generously.

9

Spoon the garlic and bean butter over the gnudi, then serve with the rest of the Parmesan for grating.

Scallops with Chorizo & Chickpeas

Preparation time: 20 minutes
Cooking time: 5 minutes
Serves 4 as a main or 6 as a starter

Despite what people say, sea scallops don't take much skill to cook—just remember to get the pan nice and hot and look for the signs I give you in the recipe. The rest of the dish can be made ahead of time, so then all you need to do is tear some good bread and pour the rest of the sherry.

---

4 oz (120 g) chorizo sausages, preferably fresh ones

1 onion

2 cloves garlic

9 oz (250 g) ripe cherry tomatoes

14 oz (400 g) canned chickpeas, drained

12 large sea scallops (I like mine with the corals still attached)

1 pinch smoked paprika

3 tbsp dry sherry (manzanilla or amontillado) or dry white wine

1 handful fresh flat-leaf parsley

sea salt and freshly ground black pepper

extra-virgin olive oil and crusty bread to serve (optional)

1

Cut the chorizo into small pieces. Heat a large skillet or shallow frying pan, then add the chorizo and cook for about 5 minutes, or until golden and surrounded with red oil. Finely chop the onion and thinly slice the garlic while you wait.

2

When the chorizo is ready, transfer to bowl. Spoon away the excess fat from the pan into another bowl, leaving about 2 tablespoons behind. If your chorizo didn't ooze that much, then add some olive oil. Add the onions and garlic to the pan and toss to coat.

3

Cook gently for 10 minutes, until softened. Meanwhile, cut the cherry tomatoes in half. Add to the onions with the chickpeas and crisped chorizo and cook for a couple of minutes until the tomatoes start to soften. Season to taste, then tip everything into a bowl. This can be done a few hours ahead and kept covered in the fridge, if you like. Wipe out the pan with paper towels.

4

Dry the scallops on paper towels, as any excess water will prevent them from caramelizing properly in the pan. Trim away the white sinewy part, then season with salt, pepper, and a little smoked paprika.

BUYING SCALLOPS
Select scallops that are creamy-looking rather than bright white. Very white scallops are likely to have been soaked in water, so they will sweat rather than caramelize. Choose hand-dived scallops, as scallop dredging is unsustainable and causes great damage to the sea bed.

5

Heat the pan over medium-high heat, then add a splash of the reserved chorizo oil (or olive oil). Let the oil heat for 30 seconds, then add the scallops, spacing them evenly. The first scallop should sizzle immediately as it hits the pan. After 2 minutes, you will see the heat creeping up the sides and a skirt of golden brown around the bottom. Lift one of the scallops. If it comes away from the pan easily and is golden and caramelized, turn it over and repeat with the rest. Cook for 1 minute more, then remove from the pan.

6

Keep the heat high, return the chickpea mixture to the pan, splash in the sherry or wine and cook for 2 minutes, shaking the pan now and again, until warmed through. Return the scallops to the pan and nestle them into the saucy chickpeas.

7

Roughly chop the flat-leaf parsley, sprinkle it over the pan, then drizzle with a little extra-virgin olive oil. Serve with good crusty bread.

Seafood Risotto

Preparation time: 25 minutes
Cooking time: 18 minutes
Serves 4–6

Making a really good seafood risotto is all about preparation, and it's a lot easier than you might suspect. Using the shells and heads from the shrimp (prawns) to make your own broth (stock) saves waste and adds great depth of flavor to the dish. Cooking the seafood in the broth ahead of time ensures you'll be relaxed and ready to concentrate on stirring the rice to creamy perfection.

18 large uncooked shrimp (prawns),
   shells and heads on
2 tbsp olive oil
2 onions
1 fennel bulb
6 tbsp (80 g) unsalted butter
2 cloves garlic
2 cups (400 g) risotto rice,
   preferably carnaroli
¾ cup (175 ml) dry white wine
a small pinch saffron threads, about
   20 (optional but worth the cost)
5 oz (150 g) small squid, about
   3 big tubes, with tentacles (ask
   your fish supplier to clean them
   and remove any cartilage)
1 lb 2 oz (500 g) mussels and clams
1 small handful fresh flat-leaf parsley
1 lemon
sea salt and freshly ground
   black pepper

1

1
Remove the heads and shells from the shrimp (prawns). To do this, take one shrimp and pinch it directly behind the head, then twist the body away. Put the head into a pan. Peel the shell away from the body using your thumb, and leave the tail on. Add the shell to the pan. Repeat with all of the shrimp.

2
Large shrimp like this often have a dark line running through their body, which is best removed. Use a toothpick or the tip of a small knife to poke a hole into the back of the shrimp, then pull out the blackish thread and discard. Chill the shrimp until needed. Cut the squid into rings.

PREPARING SHRIMP
Any good fish supplier will prepare the shrimp for you, and supply the heads and shells too. Alternatively, use uncooked peeled shrimp for the recipe and add ready-made fish broth (stock).

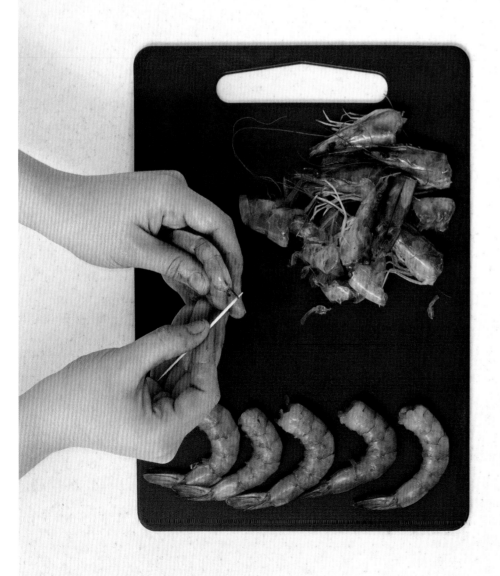

2

3

To make the broth, add 1 tablespoon oil to the pan with the heads and shells, then cook over high heat for a few minutes until they turn pink all over and take on a tinge of gold.

4

Pour in 6¼ cups (1.5 litres) water, then cover and simmer for 10 minutes while you get on with the rest of the preparation.

5

Finely chop the onions and fennel. Heat a large pan over medium heat, then add the remaining oil and 2 tablespoons (25 g) of the butter. Once melted, add the onion and fennel and cook gently for 10 minutes, until softened and translucent. While you wait, crush the garlic, then add it to the pan.

3

4

5

6

7

6

Turn the heat to medium, pour in the rice, stir until coated in the oil, then cook for 2 minutes, or until the grains start to look a little translucent around the edges. Pour in the wine, then let it bubble until most of it has evaporated. This will happen quite quickly. Take the pan from the heat for a few moments while you cook the seafood.

7

Strain the shrimp broth (stock) into a clean pan, discarding the shells and heads. Keep the broth on a gradual simmer and stir in the saffron. Add the peeled shrimp, simmer for 2 minutes, or until pink all over, then lift out with a slotted spoon and onto a plate. Repeat with the squid rings and tentacles (it will take just a few seconds to cook and turn white), then the mussels and clams. Wait for the shells to open up before lifting them out of the broth. Set the seafood aside and keep the broth bubbling gently, covered with a lid. Discard any mussels or clams that remain closed.

PREPARING MUSSELS
AND CLAMS
Give mussels and clams a good wash in cold water, then pull away the greenish-brown "beards" from the mussels. Throw away any with broken shells, plus any that don't close after a good sharp tap on the work surface. You can remove barnacles by scraping gently with a knife. Put the clams into a deep bowl of cold water and leave for half an hour or so—this will encouage them to expel any trapped sand.

8

Return the rice pan to the heat, then add a ladle of the hot broth and stir until the rice has absorbed it. Keep an eye on the temperature: if it's too hot the broth will bubble and evaporate away instead of being absorbed by the rice.

9

Continue adding the broth little by little, until the rice becomes plump and surrounded with creamy sauce. When it's ready, the rice should be just tender, without any chalkiness—taste a bit to find out. You may not need to add all the broth—somewhere between 5½–6¼ cups (1.3–1.5 litres) is normal, depending on the rice—and this will take 16–18 minutes. When you've added the last ladle of broth, don't let it absorb, but rather keep the risotto a little soupy. Season with salt and pepper to taste and take the pan from the heat.

10

Gently stir in the cooked seafood and the remaining butter in small pieces. Put a lid on and let the risotto rest for 2 minutes. The butter will melt into the rice, making it even creamier. Roughly chop the parsley and cut the lemon into wedges while you wait.

11

If you think the risotto needs loosening further, stir in a ladleful more of the broth. The rice should be loose and creamy rather than thick and stodgy. Serve the risotto in bowls, topped with a little parsley, a lemon wedge and more black pepper.

Pulled Pork Sharing Plate

Preparation time: 30 minutes
Cooking time: about 2 hours
Serves 4–6, easily doubled

Here's my version of pork carnitas, a fun and tasty Mexican meal to share with relaxed company and a few beers. It's aromatic more than spicy, so add some chopped fresh chile to the salsa if you like things hotter.

2 tbsp extra-virgin olive oil

2¼ lb (1 kg) pork shoulder, boned and cut into very large chunks (ask your butcher to do this)

2 red onions

2 cloves garlic

1 tbsp ground cumin

1 tbsp ground coriander

1 tsp hot paprika (or add ½ teaspoon chili powder to normal paprika)

1 tsp ground cinnamon

1 tbsp dried oregano

4 tbsp cider or white wine vinegar

1 tbsp tomato paste (purée)

2 limes

14 oz (400 g) canned black beans, drained (or use pinto or red kidney beans)

2 ripe avocados

1 bunch fresh cilantro (coriander)

sea salt and freshly ground black pepper

flour or corn tortillas, to serve

1

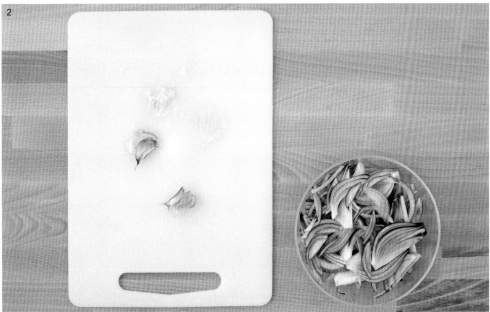

1

Preheat the oven to 325°F (160°C/ Gas Mark 3). Put a flameproof Dutch oven (casserole) over medium-high heat and add a spoonful of the oil. Season the pork with salt and pepper, then add half of it to the pan, spacing it out well. Turn the meat every few minutes, until deep golden all over. If it doesn't release itself from the pan easily, then leave it and try again in a minute or so. Set the first batch aside on a plate, then brown the second, adding more oil if needed.

2

While the pork browns, thinly slice both onions and crush the garlic.

3

Lift the second batch of meat from the pan. Turn the heat down, add half of the onion and all of the garlic, then soften in the remaining fat for 5 minutes.

4

Stir in the spices and oregano until fragrant, then add the vinegar and tomato paste (purée) and return the meat to the pan. It will smell pretty vinegary at this point, but stick with it. Pour in 1¾ cups (450 ml) water or enough to come halfway up the top pieces of meat. Cover the pan, leaving a small gap for the steam to escape, then put into the oven and cook for 2 hours.

GET AHEAD
Cook the pork up to 2 days ahead if you like, and keep chilled. The flavors will improve, and it will also be easy to lift off the excess fat.

5

While the pork cooks, prepare the accompaniments. Put the remaining sliced onion into a bowl. Add the juice of 1 lime and a pinch of salt, mix, then let steep in the fridge. The onion will become more and more pink.

6

For the salsa, put the beans into a bowl. Cut the avocados in half, then remove the pits (stones). Slice criss-crossed lines in the flesh, cutting down to, but not through, the skin, then scoop them into the bowl. Squeeze in the rest of the lime juice, stir, then season with salt and pepper. Roughly chop the cilantro (coriander) and sprinkle it over the top, so it is ready to stir in later. Chill until needed.

7

When the pork is ready, it will be very tender and soft enough to cut easily with a spoon. If it isn't ready, return to the oven and cook for 30 minutes more. Transfer the meat to a board or plate. Spoon off any excess fat from the pan, then simmer the sauce down until thick and tasty. Taste it for seasoning, then set aside.

8

Warm the tortillas according to the package instructions. Shred the pork using 2 forks, then put it into a serving dish. You can either mix it with the sauce, or serve the sauce separately. Pile the meat and sauce onto the tortillas with some salsa and onions, then wrap and enjoy immediately.

Roasted Summer Vegetable & Ricotta Lasagna

Preparation time: 1 hour 15 minutes
Cooking time: 30 minutes
Serves 6

Summer's answer to a full-on meaty lasagna, this ricotta and zucchini (courgette) combination is simple to put together and ideal for a relaxed meal in the garden. If you don't have time to make your own roasted tomato and bell pepper sauce, then use about 2 cups (500 ml) from a jar.

---

10 large plum or round ripe
   tomatoes, about 2¼ lb (1 kg)

3 red bell peppers

1 handful fresh oregano

6 tbsp extra-virgin olive oil

2 stems celery

1 onion

2 cloves garlic

5 zucchini (courgettes)

1 lb 2 oz (500 g) ricotta

4 tbsp mascarpone cheese
   (optional)

2 oz (50 g) Parmesan, or other tasty
   hard cheese such as Cheddar

1 whole nutmeg, for grating

about 6 fresh lasagna sheets—the
   exact number will depend on the
   size of your baking dish

1 handful pine nuts

sea salt and freshly ground
   black pepper

fresh salad, to serve (optional)

1

2

3

4

5

1

Preheat the oven to 400°F (200°C/ Gas Mark 6). Reserve two tomatoes then cut the rest in half. Peel the skins from the bell peppers using a vegetable peeler, then cut the peppers in half and remove the seeds and white membranes. Don't worry about peeling any fiddly bits you can't get to, this just helps the bell peppers to cook more quickly and avoid messy peeling later on.

2

Spread the tomatoes and peppers, cut side up, over 2 baking sheets (nonstick is best, if you have them). Sprinkle with some of the oregano leaves and plenty of salt and pepper. Drizzle with 3 tablespoons of the oil, then roast for 45–60 minutes, or until softened, golden and starting to shrink.

3

While the tomatoes and peppers roast, continue with the zucchini (courgette) layer. Finely chop the celery and onion.

4

Heat the remaining oil in a large skillet or frying pan, add the celery and onion, season with salt and pepper, then cover with a lid and let soften gently for 10 minutes. Covering the pan like this will part-steam the vegetables and is the best way to get celery to sweeten and soften quickly. Thinly slice the garlic and coarsely grate the zucchini. When the vegetables have softened, turn up the heat and stir in the zucchini.

5

Cook for 5 minutes, stirring often, until the zucchini is bright green and the pan is fairly dry. Stir in the garlic, cook for a minute more, then remove the pan from the heat.

6

Stir in two-thirds of the ricotta, all the mascarpone, if using, and half of the Parmesan, then season to taste with salt, pepper, and ¼ teaspoon finely grated nutmeg.

7

When the tomatoes and bell peppers are ready, put them into a food processor or use an immersion (stick) blender and process to a thick sauce. Slice the reserved tomatoes.

8

Build the lasagna. Start by spooning half the zucchini into a large baking dish. Top with a layer of lasagna sheets, then spoon half of the tomato sauce over them. Repeat the layers, finishing with tomato sauce. Cover with the sliced tomatoes, remaining ricotta, then the pine nuts and more oregano. It can be covered with plastic wrap (clingfilm) and chilled for up to 24 hours at this point.

USING DRIED LASAGNA SHEETS
Fresh lasagna sheets are quicker to cook and easy to use, but to use dried lasagna, simply bring a large pan of water to a boil, then add the sheets and stir. Boil for about 5 minutes, until softened but not cooked through. Lift out and drain, then toss with a little oil. Use as above.

9

Bake the lasagna until golden and bubbling at the edges. This will only take about 30 minutes if you have followed all the steps consecutively, as most of the layers will still be warm. If cooking from cold, add 15 minutes to the cooking time, covering with aluminum foil until halfway through. Serve with a fresh salad.

Fragrant Chicken with Quinoa Salad

Preparation time: 15 minutes, plus marinating if you like
Cooking time: 35 minutes
Serves 6–8

Fresher than a tagine, but with the same exotic North African aromas, this hearty salad is one of the easiest ways to feed a crowd. Set the platter down, perhaps with a bowl of thick yogurt on the side, and let everyone dig in.

10 pieces of chicken: 4 drumsticks, 4 thighs and 2 breasts is a good combination
2 cloves garlic
2 tbsp ras el hanout spice mixture
1 tsp chili flakes
4 tbsp vegetable or sunflower oil
2 onions
1²⁄₃ cups (300 g) quinoa
2½ cups (600 ml) vegetable or chicken broth (stock)
11 oz (300 g) green beans
2 limes (you'll need 4 tbsp juice)
1 tbsp honey
2 tbsp walnut oil
3 heads red radicchio (chicory)
3 tbsp pomegranate molasses
1 large bunch fresh cilantro (coriander)
½ cup (50 g) pistachios, walnuts, or almonds
sea salt and freshly ground black pepper

1

2

3

4

1
Slash the chicken pieces through the skin a few times, then spread out in a large roasting pan.

2
Crush the garlic. Mix half of the garlic, all the ras el hanout, chili flakes and 2 tablespoons of the oil with plenty of salt and pepper, then rub it all over the chicken pieces. If you have time, let the chicken marinate for 30 minutes, or even overnight in the fridge.

RAS EL HANOUT
This is a heady mixture of spices, normally containing cinnamon, ginger, cumin, coriander, cardamom, allspice, and paprika, among others, and often perfumed with rose petals. For a good home-made alternative, mix 1 teaspoon each ground cinnamon, cumin, sweet smoked paprika, ground coriander, and ground ginger, plus ½ teaspoon ground black pepper.

3
For the salad, thinly slice the onions. Heat 1 tablespoon oil in a large pan, then add the onions and cook over medium heat, stirring often, until softened and golden.

4
Pour in the quinoa and broth (stock), then bring to a boil.

WHAT'S QUINOA?
Quinoa is a nutritious whole grain and a great alternative to rice or couscous. In this recipe I cook it with broth and softened onions in a covered pan, so that it plumps up and absorbs all of the flavor—much like the way rice is cooked in Greece and the Middle East. You can also boil, then drain it. The grain is cooked when the little germ (which looks like a tail) pops out and the grains are tender but not mushy.

5

Cover the pan with a lid and simmer the quinoa for 10 minutes. While it simmers, trim, then chop the beans into short lengths.

6

After the quinoa has cooked for 10 minutes, add the beans to the pan, cover and cook for another 5 minutes until the beans are steamed and the quinoa cooked through. Spread the quinoa and beans over a platter or large baking sheet to help them to cool as quickly as possible. Turn with a fork occasionally as they cool.

7

Make the dressing for the quinoa. Squeeze the lime juice, then mix with the honey, walnut oil, remaining garlic, and some salt and pepper. Separate as many radicchio (chicory) leaves as you can, then roughly chop the inner leaves.

8

When you're ready to cook, preheat the oven to 400°F (200°C/Gas Mark 6). Put the chicken in to roast for 20 minutes, skin side up. After 20 minutes, take the breast portions out then return the drumsticks and thighs to the oven, as they will need longer cooking. Cook for another 15 minutes, then return the breasts to the pan, drizzle the pomegranate molasses over all the pieces, then give everything a quick blast in the oven until the molasses is bubbling.

9

Just before serving, roughly chop the cilantro (coriander). Toss the cilantro, radicchio (chicory) and dressing through the cooled quinoa. Top with the chicken (slice the breast meat), then pour the cooking juices over the meat. Sprinkle with the nuts and serve.

Lemon-Roasted Fish & Slow-Cooked Beans

Preparation time: 15 minutes
Cooking time: 30 minutes
Serves 6, easily halved

Like many of the recipes in this book, I'd like you to think of this not only as a dish as a whole, but also a great way to cook two things—fish that goes with almost anything and Turkish-style beans that also pair beautifully with roasted meat, rice or polenta.

---

2 onions

2 cloves garlic

6 tbsp extra-virgin olive oil

1 bay leaf

about 2¼ lb (1 kg) green or
    runner beans

1 lb 5 oz (600 g) canned chopped
    plum tomatoes

3 tbsp tomato paste (purée)

a pinch of sugar, or to taste

1½ cups (350 ml) vegetable or
    chicken broth (stock)

6 thick white fish fillets, skin on

1 organic (unwaxed) lemon

1 handful fresh marjoram
    or oregano

sea salt and freshly ground
    black pepper

1

Prepare the Turkish-style beans first. They can be cooked a day ahead and reheated, if you like. Chop the onions and thinly slice the garlic. Heat 5 tablespoons of the oil in a large pan, then add the onions, garlic, bay leaf, and a good pinch of salt.

2

Cook for 10 minutes over low heat, until softened and translucent.

3

Trim the beans while the onions are cooking, then shred them fairly thinly. Sometimes runner beans can be a bit stringy along the side edges. If you need to remove any strings, I find the simplest thing is to run a vegetable peeler along each edge a few times.

4

Add the beans, tomatoes, tomato paste (purée), sugar, and broth to the pan and stir well. Simmer gently for 30 minutes. The tomato sauce will need to be thick and rich by the end of cooking, but if the pan starts to look too dry at any point, just add a splash of water.

SLOW-COOKING VEGETABLES?
It's unusual these days to advocate cooking green vegetables until soft and tender, but this is a classic method in Turkish cooking, infusing the beans with the taste of rich tomato and olive oil. They're delicious cold, too.

5

Double-check that all the scales have been removed from the fish. To do this, run the back of your knife back and forth across the skin. Any remaining scales will fall off easily.

6

Preheat the oven to 425°F (220°C/Gas Mark 7). Rinse the fish, then dry with paper towels. Slash the fish a couple of times on the skin side, then season with salt and pepper. Zest the lemon, then slice thinly. Lightly oil a large baking pan, spread the slices over the pan, then sit the fish on top. Sprinkle with a handful of torn herbs and the lemon zest, then drizzle with the remaining olive oil.

Roast the fish for about 15 minutes, or until the flesh has turned white and flakes easily. The skin should open out a bit where it has been slashed.

ROASTING FISH
This is the ideal way to roast fish. As the lemon slices infuse through the flesh as it cooks, the juices create steam to keep the flesh moist and the slices protect the fish from the direct heat of the pan. If you'd like to try cooking whole fish for this recipe, then choose something not too large, such as a small bass or sea bream. Ask the fish supplier to clean and scale the fish for you. Stuff the cavity of the fish with lemon slices and more herbs, then roast for 20 minutes, or until the flesh flakes easily at the backbone.

7

When the beans are ready, they will be tender and the sauce thickened and rich. Check the seasoning.

8

Serve the beans topped with the fish and enjoy with crusty bread, or even some simple couscous or rice.

Easy Mezze

Preparation time: 20 minutes
Cooking time: 10 minutes
Serves 6 to share as an appetizer,
easily doubled

This is a little fusion of some of
my favorite nibbles—eggplant
(aubergine) dip, dukkah, melon salad
and flatbread—all easy to prepare
and colorful to bring to the table.
If you haven't tried melon with feta
before, then get ready for a taste
sensation—the salty cheese and
the cold, clean-tasting melon are
so refreshing.

extra-virgin olive oil, for brushing,
   drizzling, and dipping
3 eggplants (aubergines)
2 cloves garlic
2/3 cup (150 g) thick Greek yogurt
1 organic (unwaxed) lemon
1 bunch fresh dill
1 tbsp sesame seeds
½ cup (50 g) toasted chopped hazelnuts
1 tsp paprika
1 tsp garam masala
½ watermelon
3½ oz (100 g) feta cheese
1 handful fresh mint
sea salt and freshly ground
   black pepper
flatbreads or pita bread to serve
   (see page 268)

1
Preheat the broiler (grill) and lightly oil a large baking sheet or pan. Cut the eggplants (aubergines) in half, then score deep cuts into the flesh. Put onto the sheet.

2
Broil (grill) the eggplants for 10 minutes on each side until the flesh is very soft and mushy. Meanwhile, crush the garlic.

3
Use a spoon to scoop the eggplant flesh into the bowl of a food processor.

4
Now add the yogurt, garlic, the zest of the lemon, and half of its juice. Process until smooth, then take out the blade and snip in the dill leaves. Stir to combine. Season with salt and pepper to taste.

NO FOOD PROCESSOR?
If you don't have a food processor, you could use an immersion (stick) blender, or simply chop the cooked eggplant and mix with the rest of the ingredients in a bowl.

5

Make the dukkah. Pour the sesame seeds into a hot pan, then stir around for a few minutes until golden and toasted. Transfer the seeds to a bowl, then mix with the nuts, paprika and garam masala. Season with plenty of salt.

WHAT IS DUKKAH
Dukkah is an aromatic Egyptian side dish, made with plenty of mixed spices and crushed nuts. I used garam masala as the spicy base, a great cheat ingredient that is a ready-toasted blend of cumin, coriander and other spices usually used to make dukkah, in one easy pot. To eat, tear a bite-size piece of bread, dip it into the oil and then into the dukkah. It makes a great crust for lamb cutlets too.

6

Cut the watermelon in half, then into thin wedges. Slice the melon down to the skin at ½-inch (1-cm) intervals. Slide the knife under the flesh to release triangular pieces from the skin.

7

Put the melon onto a plate, then crumble the feta over it and sprinkle with the mint leaves. Drizzle with a little oil and season with salt and pepper.

8

Serve the eggplant dip, dukkah, and melon salad together, with a dish of olive oil and flatbreads for dipping.

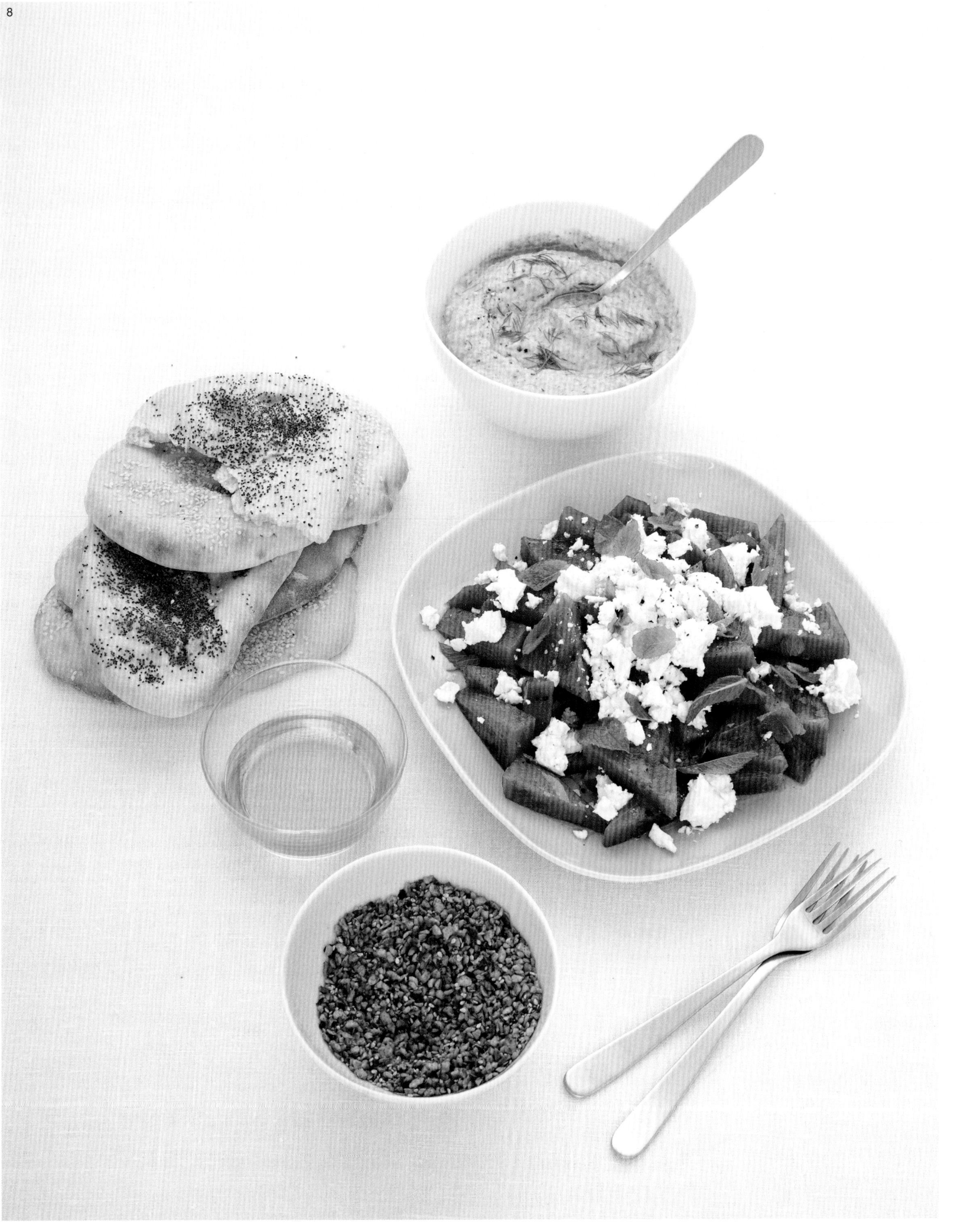

Sticky BBQ Chicken & Slaw

Preparation time: 40 minutes,
plus marinating
Cooking time: 40 minutes
Serves 6, easily doubled

For chicken pieces that are tender
right through, I always cook them
ahead of time in the oven, then finish
them on the grill (barbecue). That way
the coals can impart a char-grilled
taste, and the chicken will fall off the
bone. It also means you'll have more
room on the grill. The sauce is ideal
for dipping sausages and wings and
is just a little bit addictive.

12 chicken pieces: thighs and
    drumsticks are best, skin on
2 tbsp paprika
1 handful fresh thyme
2 tsp sea salt
½ tsp freshly ground black pepper
1 tsp chili powder
½ cup (120 g) dark brown
    (dark muscovado) sugar
⅔ cup (150 ml) tomato ketchup
1 tsp Tabasco sauce
2 tbsp Worcestershire sauce
1 small red cabbage
2 crisp, tangy apples
1 onion
⅔ cup (150 g) mayonnaise
2 tbsp cider vinegar
1 generous tsp black onion
    (kalonji) seeds
sea salt and freshly ground
    black pepper

1
Slash the chicken pieces with a sharp knife, going right down to the bone. This will help the smoky taste to sink into the chicken and will also help the heat get into the meat as it cooks.

2
Mix the paprika, thyme, salt, pepper, chili powder, and 3 tablespoons of the sugar in a large bowl or food storage bag, then add the chicken and rub well. Leave the chicken in the rub for at least 1 hour—ideally up to 12 hours in the fridge.

3
Preheat the oven to 350°F (180°C/ Gas Mark 4). Make the barbecue sauce. Mix the remaining sugar, ketchup, Tabasco, and Worcestershire sauce until smooth. This can be made several days ahead, and will keep in the fridge for at least 2 weeks.

4
Spread out the chicken in a large roasting pan. Roast the chicken for 30 minutes, until cooked all the way through (make a cut with a sharp knife to check—the meat may still be a little pink, as it is darker leg meat; however, it should not be bloody). This can be done several hours ahead, if it helps—cool the chicken and put into the fridge as soon as possible.

5

For the slaw, cut the cabbage into wedges, remove any very hard bits from the central core, then thinly slice.

6

Thinly slice the onion and the apples (no need to peel the apples first), and add to the cabbage in a large bowl.

7

Mix the mayonnaise and vinegar together to make the dressing.

8

Toss the dressing into the slaw, season with salt and pepper to taste, then sprinkle with the onion seeds. The slaw can be made up to a day ahead.

9

Before you begin the final cooking, check that your charcoal is glowing white hot, or your gas grill (barbecue) is preheated to 400°F (200°C). Place the chicken onto the grill and cook for 10 minutes, turning regularly, until charred and sizzling and hot through to the middle. Spoon or brush some of the sauce over it, then serve the chicken with the slaw and the rest of the sauce for spooning.

IF IT RAINS
Preheat the oven to 425°F (220°C/ Gas Mark 7). Roast the chicken for another 10 minutes in the oven until sizzling and dark, then finish with the sauce as before.

Lamb Kofte with Tzatziki

Preparation time: 40 minutes,
plus chilling
Cooking time: 10–15 minutes
Serves 6, easily doubled

Kofte (classic lamb meatballs served all over the Middle East) make a great alternative to burgers, are just as economical to make and as simple to cook. This mixture is quite highly spiced—in an aromatic rather than hot way—and tempered beautifully with a scoop of cooling tzatziki (cucumber yogurt sauce).

2 onions

2 cloves garlic

¼ cup (50 g) dried apricots

1 bunch fresh mint

1¾ lb (800 g) good-quality ground
   (minced) lamb

1 tbsp ground cumin

1 tsp chili powder

1 tbsp dried thyme

1 egg

2 cucumbers

1⅓ cups (300 g) creamy plain yogurt

6 flatbreads (see page 268), or
   use ready-made pita bread,
   to serve

sea salt and freshly ground
   black pepper

1

Finely chop the onions and crush the garlic, then finely chop the apricots and half of the mint.

2

Put the ground (minced) lamb into a large bowl with the onions, garlic, apricots, chopped mint, cumin, chili powder, thyme, and egg. Season generously with ½ teaspoon each salt and pepper.

3

Mix everything together with your hands until evenly combined. If you want to check the seasoning of the kofte, you can pan fry a little piece of the mixture and add more seasoning to your taste. With slightly damp hands, shape the kofte mixture into 25–30 walnut-size balls. Cover and chill for at least 30 minutes, or for up to 2 days.

4

To make the tzatziki, peel the cucumbers, then scoop out the seeds using a teaspoon. Leaving the seeds in will lead to a watery sauce. Thinly slice or grate the flesh.

5

Mix the cucumber with the yogurt. Tear in the remaining mint leaves, then season to taste with salt and pepper.

6

Before you begin cooking, check that the your charcoal is glowing white hot, or your gas grill (barbecue) is preheated to 400°F (200°C). Cook the kofte for about 10 minutes, turning often, until dark golden all over and hot through to the middle. When ready, serve the kofte with the tzatziki and flatbreads.

IF IT RAINS
Cook the kofte in a large skillet or frying pan—you may need to do this in two batches. Alternatively, cook on a rack under a hot broiler (grill).

Lemon & Herb Pork with Fennel & Mint Salad

Preparation time: 30 minutes,
plus marinating
Cooking time: 12–15 minutes
Serves 4–6, easily doubled

Pork tenderloin is ideal for cooking on the grill (barbecue) as it's so lean and tender and only takes a few minutes to cook. When you thread the skewers, try not to pack everything too tightly. The heat needs to get all around the pork, to avoid overcooking the outside before the middle is done.

2 pork tenderloins, about
    1½ lb (700 g) in total
2 fat cloves garlic
2 organic (unwaxed) lemons
4 tbsp white wine
6 tbsp extra-virgin olive oil,
    plus extra for greasing
2 tsp dried thyme
2 tsp fennel seeds
36 small new potatoes,
    about 1 lb 5 oz (600 g)
3 fennel bulbs
2 oz (50 g) chunk pecorino or
    Parmesan cheese
1 bunch fresh mint
sea salt and freshly ground
    black pepper

1

Cut the pork tenderloins into large bite-size cubes, and trim away any silvery pieces of membrane.

2

Crush the garlic and finely grate the zest from the lemons. Put the pork into a large food storage bag or non-metallic bowl, then add the garlic, zest, wine, 4 tablespoons of the oil, thyme and fennel seeds. Stir well to coat, then seal or cover and let marinate in the fridge for at least 2 hours, or up to 24 hours.

3

Put the potatoes into a pan of cold, salted water, then bring to a boil. Cook for 15 minutes or until tender. Drain and set aside. The potatoes can be cooked and cooled up to a day ahead.

4

The salad can be prepared a few hours ahead too. Halve, trim, then thinly slice the fennel bulbs. Shave the cheese using a vegetable peeler and keep everything covered in the fridge until needed.

5

Before you begin cooking, check that your charcoal is glowing white hot or that your gas grill (barbecue) is preheated to 400°F (200°C). Take the meat from the marinade, thread the meat and potatoes alternately onto 6 metal skewers, and season generously. To get ahead, assemble the skewers a few hours beforehand and keep in the fridge. Ensure that the skewers have a few minutes at room temperature before cooking.

METAL OR WOODEN SKEWERS
If you use your grill a lot, a set of metal skewers is a sound investment. Wooden skewers should be soaked in cold water for at least 30 minutes before cooking (minus the meat of course) to minimize scorching.

6

Cook the skewers for 12–15 minutes, turning four times during cooking until golden all over, firm when pressed, and no longer pink in the middle. Take care with this leaner cut of pork, as it can easily dry out. While you wait, squeeze the juice of one lemon and cut the other into 6 wedges. Toss the juice and 2 tablespoons oil into the fennel salad, season and scatter with torn mint leaves. Serve with the skewers and lemon wedges for squeezing.

Spicy Mackerel with Orange & Radish Salad

Preparation time: 20 minutes,
plus marinating
Cooking time: 6–10 minutes
Serves 6, easily doubled

Oily fish like mackerel and sardines are delicious with hot spices. Try them with harissa or curry paste, which cut through the richness of the flesh. Whole fish cook well on the grill (barbecue), but there are a few tricks to getting the best result. See page 13 for more information about cooking fish.

6 small or 3 large fresh mackerel —
    ask your fish supplier to clean (gut)
    them and to remove the heads
1 tbsp harissa paste
2 tbsp extra-virgin olive oil, plus
    extra for greasing
3 large or 6 small oranges
11 oz (300 g) radishes
1 red onion
2 tbsp sherry vinegar
1 bunch fresh flat-leaf parsley
sea salt and freshly ground
    black pepper

1
Rinse the fish under cold running water to remove any blood, then dry with paper towels. Slash the flesh 3–4 times on each side for small fish or 5 times for large fish.

2
Mix the harissa paste, 1 tablespoon of oil and plenty of salt and pepper, then rub this all over the fish. Marinate in the fridge for a few minutes (or up to 3 hours), while you make the salad.

ABOUT HARISSA
This feisty paste of dried red chiles, garlic, and spices is originally from Tunisia, but can be found in specialty markets and some supermarkets. As an alternative, stir 1 tablespoon olive oil, 1 crushed garlic clove, and ½ teaspoon each ground cumin and coriander into 1 tablespoon chili paste or sauce.

3

Cut the top and bottom from each orange, then, using a serrated knife, cut away the skin and pith. Take care to follow the line of the orange flesh, so that you don't trim too much of it. Cut into thin slices.

4

Thinly slice the radishes and the red onion. Toss in a serving dish with the oranges, vinegar, and remaining olive oil. Season with salt and pepper.

5

Before you begin cooking, check that your charcoal is glowing white hot, or your gas grill (barbecue) is preheated to 400°F (200°C). Use a heat-resistant brush to oil the grill rack, then cook small fish for 3 minutes or large fish for 5–6 minutes on each side, until charred and cooked through. If your grill has a lid, then you can use it here. Test with a knife—the flesh at the backbone should flake easily. Toss the parsley leaves through the salad, then serve with the fish.

COOKING FISH ON THE GRILL
Inevitably, some fish skin will stick to the grate. Oiling helps, but if you plan to cook a lot of fish it makes sense to invest in a grill basket for fish—a wire cage with handles that sandwiches around the fish and can be turned easily. Oil this too. Alternatively, heat a grill pan (griddle) on the grill. That way the fish flavor won't be transferred to the grate beneath.

IF IT RAINS
Preheat the broiler (grill) and cook the fish on a baking sheet for about 10 minutes, turning carefully once.

Shrimp (Prawn) & Asparagus Skewers

Preparation time: 20 minutes
Cooking time: 6–7 minutes
Makes 6 skewers,
easily doubled

Keep the shells on shrimp (prawns) for the barbecue, as they protect the meat from overcooking too quickly, and also hold in all of the tasty juices. I like to serve these skewers with a mint aïoli. With an easy hand blender method, it's a cinch to make.

12 asparagus spears, the fatter
    the better
18 large uncooked shrimp (prawns),
    with the shells on
2 eggs, at room temperature
2 lemons
1 clove garlic
1 tsp Dijon mustard
scant 1 cup (200 ml) olive oil
1 small handful fresh mint
sea salt and freshly ground
    black pepper

1
Bring a pan of salted water to a boil. Meanwhile, cut the bottom 2 inches (5 cm) from each asparagus spear, as the ends can often be a bit tough. Cut each spear into two finger-length pieces.

2
Boil the spears for just 2 minutes, then drain. Plunge into cold water to stop the cooking, then drain again.

WHY PRE-COOK?
Without a little pre-cooking, the asparagus would take far longer than the shrimp (prawns) to cook on the grill (barbecue). It also makes it easier to poke the skewers through the asparagus.

3

Thread 3 shrimp and 4 pieces of asparagus onto 6 metal skewers. Cover and chill in the fridge until needed.

4

To make the aïoli, separate the eggs (see page 61) and put the yolks into a tall pitcher (jug). Squeeze 1 lemon and roughly chop the garlic. Add the garlic, mustard, 2 tablespoons lemon juice, and the oil to the yolks.

5

Put an immersion (stick) blender to the very bottom of the pitcher, then start it running. Pull the blender very slowly from the bottom of the pitcher. As you bring the blender nearer to the top of the pitcher, the mayonnaise will thicken dramatically and you will feel a suction pulling under the blades. Add more lemon juice and salt and pepper to taste. If the mayonnaise is a bit thick but tastes lemony enough, add a splash of water and blend again. This can be made a few days in advance and kept well chilled, if you like.

6

Before you begin cooking, check that your charcoal is glowing white hot, or your gas grill (barbecue) is preheated to 400°F (200°C). Season the skewers with salt and pepper, then grill for 2–3 minutes on each side, or until the asparagus is slightly charred and the shrimp are pink all over. Quickly chop the mint and add to the mayonnaise. Cut the remaining lemon into wedges to garnish. Serve immediately with the mint aïoli.

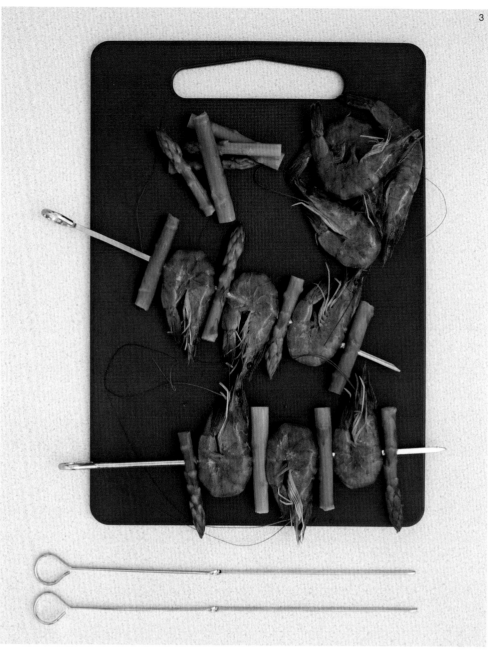

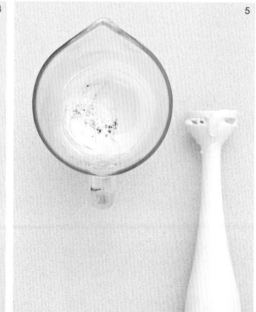

Sticky Soy Ribs with Asian Slaw

Preparation time: 20 minutes, plus marinating
Cooking time: About 3 hours
Serves 6, easily doubled

Satisfy the caveman (or woman) in you with these tender ribs, cooked until melting in the oven, then grilled to crisp and dark perfection. When buying whole racks of pork ribs or baby back beef ribs, ask for the membrane (from the back of the rack) to be removed for you.

---

1 finger-length piece fresh
   ginger
3 fat cloves garlic
4½ lb (2 kg) pork spareribs
½ cup (100 g) superfine
   (caster) sugar
1 tbsp Chinese five-spice powder
⅔ cup (150 ml) light soy sauce
2 tbsp sesame oil
1 large or 2 smaller heads
   Napa cabbage (Chinese leaf)
1 bunch scallions (spring onions)
1 fat red chile
scant ½ cup (100 ml) rice vinegar
2 tbsp sesame seeds
sea salt and freshly ground
   black pepper

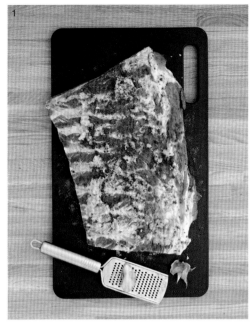

1
Finely grate the ginger and the garlic, then rub all over the ribs.

2
Put 5 tablespoons of the sugar, the five-spice powder, then the soy sauce and 1 tablespoon sesame oil into a non-metallic container or a large plastic food storage bag. Mix together, then add the ribs. Massage the marinade around the meat, then let marinate in the fridge for at least 2 hours or up to 24 hours. The longer the better.

3
Preheat the oven to 325°F (160°C/ Gas Mark 3). Lift the ribs from the marinade, then put them into a large roasting pan. Reserve the marinade. Splash a cup of water in the bottom of the pan, then cover the whole thing with a tent of aluminum foil—the ribs are going to steam until tender.

4
Bake the ribs for 2½ hours, then have a look and see how they are doing. The meat should be very tender and easy to pull away from the bones. If not, spoon some of the juices over the ribs (or add more water if the pan looks dry), then re-cover the pan and return to the oven for another 30 minutes before testing again. Smaller racks will take less time and vice versa. The ribs can be cooked and chilled ahead of time, ready to be grilled (barbecued) the next day.

USING BEEF RIBS
Beef ribs are delicious cooked this way too. They will need around 3–4 hours to tenderize in the oven, depending on their size.

5

To prepare the slaw, finely shred the Napa cabbage (Chinese leaf) and thinly slice the scallions (spring onions). Put into a large bowl, then cover and chill until needed.

6

To make the dressing, deseed and finely chop the chile, then put it into a small bowl. Mix in the vinegar, remaining sugar (about 2 tablespoons) and sesame oil, then season with a pinch of salt. Cook the sesame seeds in a pan over medium heat for a few minutes until golden and toasted, stirring often.

7

Skim the excess fat from the juices in the roasting pan (beef ribs will release a lot), then pour the juices and remaining marinade into a pan and boil until syrupy (about 10 minutes).

8

Before you begin the final cooking, check that your charcoal is glowing white hot, or your gas grill (barbecue) is preheated to 400°F (200°C). Toss the salad dressing through the slaw and set aside to let the dressing soak in. Cook the ribs for about 5 minutes on each side, until sizzling and dark golden. If you are cooking the ribs from cold, give them a little longer to be sure they're heated through. Transfer to a board, then cut into individual ribs, or portions of several. Spoon the syrupy sauce over the ribs and sprinkle with the sesame seeds. Serve with the salad.

IF IT RAINS
Finish the ribs under a hot broiler (grill) until sizzling.

Chimichurri-Style Burgers

Preparation time: 30 minutes,
plus chilling
Cooking time: under 10 minutes
Makes 8 burgers, easily halved

Chimichurri is an Argentinian
marinade or sauce, normally
spooned over char-grilled steak.
This recipe takes the essence of
the original (lots of herbs, vinegar
and spice), and combines it
with fresh tomatoes and onions
to make a tasty, spoonable salsa.

2 red onions
1 large bunch fresh flat-leaf parsley
1 large bunch fresh cilantro
   (coriander)
2¼ lb (1 kg) good-quality ground
   (minced) beef
1½ tsp dried chili flakes
1 egg
4 ripe tomatoes
2 cloves garlic
2 tbsp red wine vinegar
1 tsp superfine (caster) sugar
1 tsp dried oregano
1 tbsp olive oil
a few drops of Tabasco (optional)
mayonnaise, salad greens (leaves)
   and hamburger buns, to serve
sea salt and freshly ground
   black pepper

1

2

1
Finely chop 1 onion and half the cilantro (coriander) and parsley leaves. Put into a large bowl with the ground (minced) beef, 1 teaspoon of the chili flakes, the egg, and plenty of salt and pepper.

2
Work the ground beef and other ingredients together using your hands, until everything is well combined. Shape the meat into 8 patties, making sure they are nice and flat, then chill in the fridge for at least 30 minutes. The burgers can be made up to a day ahead.

TASTE A BIT
The beauty of making your own burgers is that you can cook a little piece to check the seasoning. Pinch off a little meat, heat a skillet or frying pan and cook for a couple of minutes. Taste, then add more seasoning if you need to. I find that burgers normally need a surprisingly large amount.

3

Make the chimichurri salsa. Halve the tomatoes, then scoop out the seeds with a spoon and discard. Finely chop the flesh. Crush the garlic and finely chop the remaining onion and herbs, including their stems if they are soft.

4

Mix the tomatoes with the garlic, onion, and herbs. Stir in the remaining chili flakes, vinegar, sugar, oregano, oil, and Tabasco. Season with salt and pepper. Although the salsa contains lots of fresh herbs, it holds up well and can be made an hour or so ahead. Keep it chilled.

5

Before you begin cooking, check that your charcoal is glowing white hot, or your gas grill (barbecue) is preheated to 400°F (200°C). Cook the burgers for 2 minutes on each side for medium rare, or 3–4 minutes on each side, for medium or well done. Split the buns and toast on the grill rack if you like. Top the bottom halves of the buns with a good spoon of mayonnaise and some salad greens (leaves). Add the burgers and spoonfuls of the chimichurri salsa to serve.

IF IT RAINS
Char-grill, broil (grill), or sauté the burgers until golden and juicy.

Goat Cheese
& Polenta Stacks

Preparation time: 30 minutes
Cooking time: about 12–15 minutes
Serves 4–6, easily halved

Vegetarian guests deserve more than
a dry old veggie burger from the
freezer, so why not make something
to make everyone's mouth water,
even the die-hard carnivores? Take
the goat cheese from the fridge a
good hour before you use it for the
best creamy texture.

6¼ cups (1.5 litres) vegetable
    broth (stock)
2 oz (50 g) Parmesan cheese or
    other strong-tasting, hard cheese
2½ cups (375 g) quick-cooking
    polenta
4 tbsp (50 g) unsalted butter
¾ cup (175 ml) extra-virgin olive oil,
    plus extra for brushing
2 cloves garlic
1 bunch fresh basil or
    flat-leaf parsley
6 large Portabello mushrooms
2–3 red bell peppers
3 x 3½-oz (100-g) ripe, rinded
    goat cheeses
2 tbsp tapenade (olive paste)
    or pesto
sea salt and freshly ground
    black pepper

1

Pour the broth (stock) into a large pan, then bring to a boil. While you wait, finely grate the Parmesan. Carefully pour the polenta into the boiling broth in a steady stream, stirring constantly with a wooden spoon, until all of the polenta has been added.

The polenta will thicken up quickly. Cook for a couple of minutes until very thick, stirring with a long-handled wooden spoon, as it will bubble and pop as it boils. Take the pan from the heat, then stir in the grated cheese, the butter, and plenty of salt and pepper. Taste a little bit—you may be surprised how much seasoning polenta can need.

2

Rub a little oil around the inside of an 8 × 12-inch (20 × 30-cm) baking pan, then pour in the polenta and smooth the top. Let cool for at least 10 minutes. It will set firm. You can do this a day ahead if you like—just keep it covered and in the fridge.

3

Make the herbed oil and prepare the vegetables. Crush the garlic and finely chop the basil. Add to a bowl with the remaining oil and season with salt and pepper.

4

If the mushroom stems are poking above the cap, then trim to cap level with a knife. Deseed, then quarter, the bell peppers. Brush the bell peppers and mushrooms with a little herbed oil.

5

Using a 4-inch (10-cm) cookie cutter (or you can use a saucer as a template to cut around), cut out 6 circles from the polenta. Cut the goat cheeses into 6 halves.

6

Before you begin cooking, check that your charcoal is glowing white hot, or your gas grill (barbecue) is preheated to 400°F (200°C). Lightly brush the polenta with a little plain oil. Cook the polenta for a couple of minutes on each side, either directly on the grill or in a grill pan (griddle) set over the grill, until golden and crisp. Set aside and keep warm.

7

Place the mushrooms and bell peppers directly on the grill rack for about 5 minutes on each side, until golden and softened. Spoon some tapenade or pesto into the middle of each circle of polenta, then top with a piece of pepper, an upturned mushroom and then a circle of goat cheese. Drizzle with more of the garlic and basil oil, then serve.

IF IT RAINS
Cook the polenta and vegetables in a grill pan (griddle), skillet, or frying pan, then stack and serve as above. Keep the polenta warm in a low oven while the vegetables cook, if you need to.

Hot Dogs with Tomato, Sage, & Onion Relish

Preparation time: about 40 minutes, plus cooling
Cooking time: about 15 minutes
Serves 6–8, easily doubled

Rather than glazing or marinating sausages, choose good-quality sausages or hot dogs and have fun with the topping instead. The quick relish doesn't need to mellow before eating and is easy to make. Try it with cheese or cold cuts too.

2 onions

1 orange (or red) bell pepper

1 crisp, tangy apple such
    as Braeburn

2 tbsp olive, vegetable or
    sunflower oil

1 tsp salt

2 cloves garlic

1 fat red chile

1 thumb-size piece of fresh ginger

6 large tomatoes, about 1 lb 2 oz
    (500 g)

scant ½ cup (50 g) raisins, golden
    raisins, or sultanas

scant ½ cup (100 ml) red wine
    vinegar

½ cup (100 g) superfine (caster)
    sugar

1 small handful fresh sage

6 or 8 large, good-quality
    pork sausages

6 or 8 hot dog or sub rolls

your choice of mustard, to serve

sea salt and freshly ground
    black pepper

1
Slice the onions, then deseed and chop the bell pepper. Core and chop the apple into small pieces.

2
Heat the oil in a large pan, then add the onions, bell pepper, apple, and salt. Cook for 10 minutes over medium heat, until softened.

MAKE A BIG BATCH
If you've a glut of tomatoes in the garden, then double the recipe. Use the largest pan you have (preferably one with sloping sides), then pack into sterilized jars and give to friends or set aside in a cool dark place to let it mature. To sterilize jars and metal lids, wash in hot soapy water, rinse, then let dry completely in a low oven. Carefully pack the relish while both it and the jars are still hot.

3

While you wait, thinly slice the garlic, finely chop the chile and peel and finely chop the ginger. Roughly chop the tomatoes and remove any tough bits of stem if needed. Keep the chile seeds in the mixture if you like a spicy relish.

PEELING GINGER
I don't normally bother to peel ginger if it's going to be grated finely, but for this purpose, peel first with a vegetable peeler. You can also scrape the peel away using a teaspoon.

4

Add the garlic, chile and ginger to the pan, cook for 2 minutes until fragrant, then add the tomatoes and raisins. Cook for 5 minutes, stirring often, then add the vinegar and cook together for 5 minutes until the onions, apple, and bell pepper are soft and the tomatoes are squashy.

5

Stir in the sugar, then keep cooking the relish, stirring very often, until the mixture looks fairly dry and sticky. Drag the spoon through it now and again—it's ready when you can draw a line in the mixture with the spoon. Finely chop the sage leaves (about 15 should do it), then stir through. Cool completely.

6

Before you begin cooking, check that your charcoal is glowing white hot, or your gas grill (barbecue) is preheated to 400°F (200°C). Cook the sausages for about 15 minutes, turning regularly, until cooked through in the middle. Split the buns, stuff with a sausage, plenty of relish and a line of mustard, if you like.

IF IT RAINS
Broil (grill) the sausages, turning frequently, until golden and cooked through.

Char-grilled Beef & Vegetables with Horseradish Cream

Preparation time: 40 minutes,
plus marinating time
Cooking time: about 1 hour,
depending on the size of the meat
Serves 6, easily doubled

Treating the grill (barbecue) like an oven is a fun way to take the Sunday roast outside. This is a recipe to make as the centerpiece of a meal. The beef will need your regular attention, but it is worth it.

---

2 whole heads of garlic

scant ½ cup (100 ml) extra-virgin
   olive oil

4 fresh beets (beetroot)

3 red onions

2 eggplants (aubergines)

3 zucchini (courgettes)

3 bell peppers, a mixture of
   colors looks good

few sprigs fresh rosemary

2 organic (unwaxed) lemons

6 tbsp sour cream or
   crème traïche

2 tsp grated horseradish or
   horseradish sauce from a jar

3⅓–4½ lb (1.5–2 kg) rib eye or
   sirloin steak

sea salt and freshly ground
   black pepper

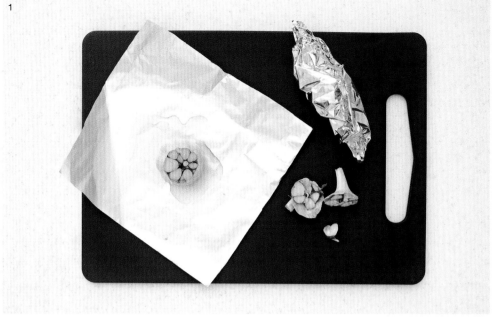

1

Prepare the vegetables ahead of time. Cut the tops from the garlic bulbs, exposing the cloves inside. Tear 2 squares of aluminum foil about 7 inches (15 cm) across, then sit a whole garlic bulb in the middle of each square. Drizzle with a little oil, then scrunch the aluminum foil to make parcels.

2

Scrub the beets (beetroot) clean (you don't need to peel them), then cut into thickish slices, about ¼ inch (5 mm). Put into a bowl.

3

Cut the onions into thick rings, removing the outer ring of skin once you've sliced them, then thickly slice the eggplants (aubergines) and zucchini (courgettes). Deseed and cut the bell peppers into chunky pieces and put in another bowl.

GETTING AHEAD
If you'd like to cook the vegetables before the grill (barbecue) is lit, then cook them on a grill pan (griddle) indoors instead. They can be cooked several hours ahead and left at room temperature.

INDIVIDUAL STEAKS
If you would prefer to cook individual steaks, about ½ inch (2 cm) thick, then simply grill for 2 minutes on each side for medium rare, adding or subtracting 30 seconds if you like your steak rare or medium. Rest for 2 minutes before serving.

4

Roughly chop the rosemary leaves. Finely grate the zest and squeeze the juice from one lemon, then mix with the rosemary and remaining oil. Toss this marinade with the beets and the other vegetables, still in their separate bowls (this will prevent the beets staining the other vegetables pink). Season generously, then let steep for at least 30 minutes and up to 24 hours. Turn the vegetables now and then, as those at the bottom of the bowl will get more of a soaking.

5

Before you begin cooking, check that your charcoal is glowing white hot, or your gas grill (barbecue) is preheated to 400°F (200°C). A grill pan (griddle) would be helpful if you have one, but is not essential. Spread the garlic parcels and one layer of vegetables over the grill basket (or directly on the rack), cooking for 3–5 minutes on each side, until softened and starting to char. The timing will depend on how hot your grill is and how far the rack is from the heat—so check frequently. Set the vegetables on a large platter as they are ready, and repeat until everything is cooked. By the time all the vegetables are cooked, the garlic should be soft and squashy.

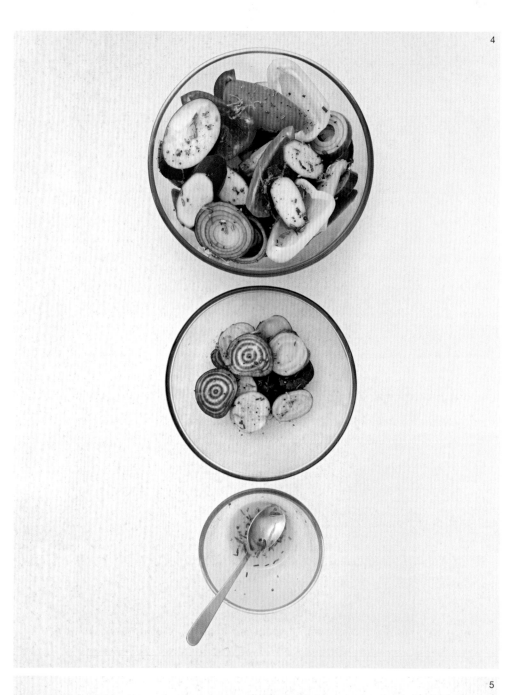

4

5

6

To make the dressing, put the cream and horseradish into a small bowl, then add a squeeze of juice from the second lemon. Squeeze the garlic out of one of the bulbs, then whisk until smooth. Season to taste.

7

When all the vegetables are ready and cooling, start cooking the beef. If you are using charcoal, then very carefully mound the coals to one side of the grill, sloping them down to one side to make hotter and cooler parts (see page 12). Rub the meat with a little oil, then season generously all over. Cook over the hottest part for 5 minutes on each side (20 minutes in total) before moving to a cooler part of the grill and covering with the lid. Cook for another 10 minutes per 1 lb (450 g) for medium rare, which for a 3¼-lb (1.5-kg) piece of meat is about 35 minutes, turning every 10 minutes. Let the dark golden beef rest on a board for 10 minutes before carving.

Carve the beef into thick slices, then serve with the vegetables, a few cloves of soft roasted garlic and spoonfuls of the horseradish cream. If you have a carving board that collects the meat juices, then give every serving a little drizzle.

Tomato & Mozzarella Salad with Gremolata

Preparation time: 10 minutes
Serves 4–6

Gremolata is a traditional Italian mixture of chopped parsley and garlic with grated lemon zest. It can be sprinkled over a salad or cooked fish, meat, or pasta. If you'd prefer a straight-up mozzarella, tomato, and basil salad, then simply tuck the leaves from a bunch of basil in among the cheese and tomato, then season with salt, pepper, and oil.

---

1 organic (unwaxed) lemon

1 small clove garlic

1 small bunch fresh flat-leaf parsley

about 1 lb 5 oz (600 g) assorted ripe
    tomatoes, at room temperature

2 large or 3 smaller balls buffalo
    mozzarella cheese

3 tbsp extra-virgin olive oil

sea salt and freshly ground
    black pepper

1
Finely grate the zest of the lemon. Finely chop the garlic and parsley leaves, then mix with the lemon zest and some salt and pepper in a bowl.

2
Slice the tomatoes and mozzarella.

HEIRLOOM TOMATOES
These bright, exotic-looking tomatoes, sometimes called "heritage," are old varieties that have come back into vogue for their very special taste and appearance. Find them in some farmers' markets, fruit and vegetable stores, and supermarkets at the peak of the tomato season.

3
Arrange the slices of tomato and cheese on a large plate, seasoning with salt and pepper as you go. Sprinkle the gremolata over the salad, then drizzle with the olive oil to serve.

Green Salad with Seeds & Croutons

Preparation time: 10 minutes
Cooking time: 2 minutes
Serves 4–6, easily doubled

A versatile, goes-with-anything kind of salad that is anything but boring. I've used ready-made croutons to keep things simple; however, if you want to make your own, toss seasoned cubes of bread with a little oil, then bake at 400°F (200°C/Gas Mark 6) until crisp and golden.

---

2 tbsp sunflower seeds

1 small clove garlic

3 tbsp olive oil

1 tbsp red or white wine vinegar

1 tsp Dijon mustard

1 tsp honey

1–2 ripe avocados

5 oz (150 g) mixed arugula (rocket), watercress, and spinach salad (or a similar mix of peppery salad greens [leaves])

a good handful ready-made croutons

sea salt and freshly ground black pepper

1

Put the sunflower seeds into a skillet or frying pan, then cook over medium heat for a few minutes, until they are toasted and sizzling. Pour onto a plate and let cool.

Crush the garlic, then put into either a small bowl or a jar. Add the oil, vinegar, mustard, and honey and a pinch of salt and pepper.

2

Whisk or shake the ingredients together to make a thickened vinaigrette.

MAKE A BATCH OF DRESSING
If you like to eat salad most days, then why not save yourself time and make a batch of dressing? Multiply the recipe and keep in a jar in the fridge for up to a week. Give it a shake before using.

3

Cut the avocado in half, remove the pit (stone), then peel off the skin. Slice thickly. If you want to do this ahead of time, toss the sliced avocado in a little lemon juice (to prevent it from going brown), then cover with plastic wrap (clingfilm) and chill.

4

Put the leaves into a large bowl, add the avocado, croutons, and the cooled seeds, then pour in the dressing. Toss well to make sure everything is coated, then serve immediately.

Potato, Bacon, & Watercress Salad

Preparation time: 10 minutes,
plus cooling
Cooking time: 15–20 minutes
Serves 4–6

I'm a big fan of the way German cooks make their potato salad. It often includes gherkins, bacon, and mustard and it's dressed while warm so that the potatoes absorb all of the flavors in the dressing. My version is a versatile side for the barbecue, picnic or dinner table.

1½ lb (700 g) small new potatoes

6 strips (rashers) bacon (dry-cured is best)

1 tbsp whole-grain mustard

1 tbsp red or white wine vinegar

2 tbsp olive oil

2 tbsp mayonnaise

4 gherkins

1 bunch scallions (spring onions)

3½ oz (100 g) watercress or arugula (rocket)

sea salt and freshly ground black pepper

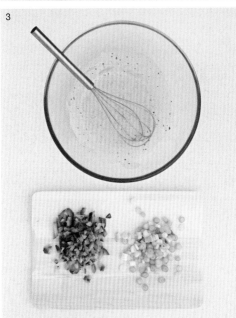

1

If some of the potatoes are on the larger side, cut them in half first. Put the potatoes into a large pan of salted water, then bring to a boil. Boil for 15–20 minutes, or until tender.

SKINS ON
I like small new potatoes for my potato salad because they don't need to be peeled before cooking. The skin acts as a helpful barrier while they are boiled, preventing them from overcooking. It provides lots of flavor and nutrients too.

2

Meanwhile, with kitchen shears (scissors), snip the bacon into bite-size pieces. Put into a skillet or frying pan over medium heat. Cook the bacon for 5 minutes or until golden and crisp. Drain the bacon on paper towel and set aside.

3

In a large bowl, mix together the mustard, vinegar, oil, and mayonnaise. Finely chop the gherkins and thinly slice the onions.

4

Drain the potatoes well, then cool for 15 minutes or so until warm. Toss with the dressing, gherkins, and onions, then let cool.

5

When ready to serve, check the seasoning of the potatoes. If they seem a little dry, add a little splash of water and stir well. Very roughly chop the watercress, stir through the salad, scatter with the bacon, then serve.

Sweet Corn with Cheesy Butter

Preparation time: 10 minutes,
plus chilling
Cooking time: 5 minutes
Serves 6, easily doubled

No one really needs a recipe for
boiling some corn, but this dish is
really about the butter, with its rich,
intense cheesiness and slight kick.
It complements the sweetness
of the corn, and is delicious on hot
potatoes too.

1 stick (120 g) unsalted butter,
   very soft
¾ oz (20 g) Parmesan or other
   sharp, very mature cheese
1 handful fresh chives
½ tsp cayenne pepper or
   hot paprika
¾ tsp English mustard powder
6 large ears of corn (sweetcorn
   cobs)
sea salt and freshly ground
   black pepper

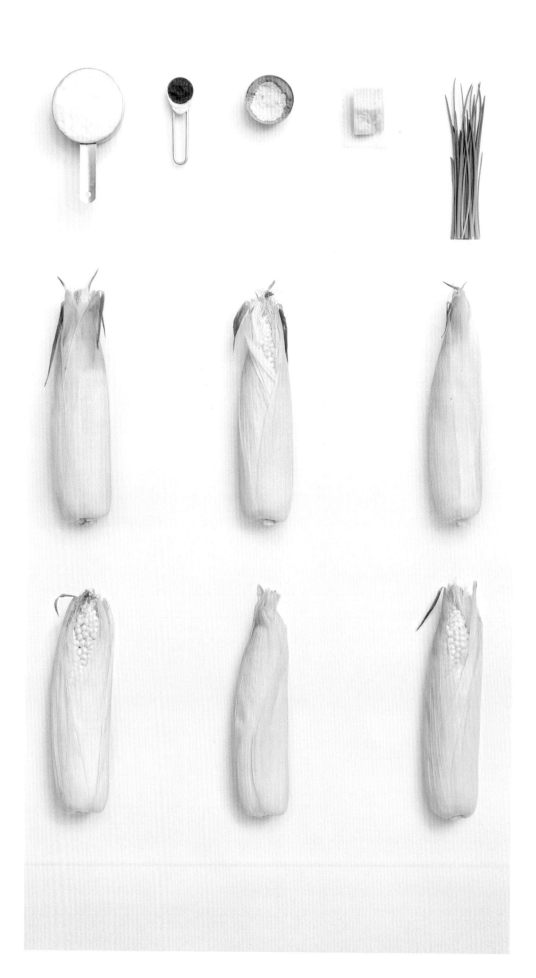

1

Put the butter into a large bowl, then beat it with a wooden spoon until evenly creamy and smooth. Finely grate the cheese and add to the bowl. Snip in half of the chives using kitchen shears (scissors), then add the cayenne or paprika, mustard powder, and ½ teaspoon salt.

2

Beat everything together until thoroughly combined. Spread a large sheet of plastic wrap (clingfilm) over the work surface, then spoon the butter onto it, in a rough log. Use a rubber spatula to get every last bit of butter from the bowl. Roll the plastic wrap around the butter, then twist it into a tight sausage. Chill for 10 minutes in the freezer until firm (or longer in the fridge, if you have time).

3

If your corn has the husks intact, then you'll need to shuck (remove) them, and pull off the strands of silk surrounding the kernels. Trim the ends. Use a serrated knife to cut each ear of corn in half. This isn't strictly necessary, but makes the corn easier to pick up later (or stretch to feed more people).

4

When ready to cook, bring a large pan of salted water to a boil, then add the corn and boil for 10 minutes, or until tender, turning them now and then so that they cook evenly. Check if the corn is ready by carefully removing one from the water. Pull out a kernel with a fork and try it. It should be sweet and crisp but not starchy-tasting.

ON THE GRILL (BARBECUE)
If you're grilling (barbecuing), the corn can be finished over the hot coals for a slightly smokier taste and charred look. I find it best to boil the corn first so that they only need a few minutes to brown here and there, saving time and space on the grill. You could even boil them ahead, cool them quickly under cold water to stop them from cooking, then drain well and chill. Reheat on the grill when you're ready.

5

When the corn is tender, drain well, then put onto a serving plate. Slice the cheesy butter and put a disc of it on top of each one—it will start to melt over the corn. Snip the rest of the chives over. Season with salt and pepper and serve.

Hasselback Sweet Potatoes

Preparation time: 10 minutes
Cooking time: 1 hour
Serves 6, easily doubled

Strictly speaking, a Hasselback potato would be a regular white potato, skin left on, flesh slashed and stuffed with bay leaves, then roasted in the oven. The idea translates wonderfully to sweet potatoes, which open out as they roast, ready to soak up lots of maple syrup, chili, lime, and sour cream.

6 large sweet potatoes
2 sprigs fresh rosemary
3 tbsp olive oil
3 tbsp maple syrup, or more
    if you like
1 tsp dried chili flakes, or
    more if you like
1 lime
6 tbsp plain or Greek yogurt, sour
    cream or crème fraîche
sea salt and freshly ground
    black pepper

1

2

3

1
Preheat the oven to 400°F (200°C/ Gas Mark 6). Cut slits in the potatoes at ½-inch (1-cm) intervals, going almost all the way through the potato.

2
Finely chop the rosemary leaves. Put the potatoes into a roasting pan. Rub the oil over them, then sprinkle with the rosemary and plenty of salt and pepper. Try and get as much of the rosemary into the potatoes as you can.

3
Bake for 1 hour, or until tender in the middle and crisp outside, and the potatoes have fanned out.

4
Just before serving, drizzle the hot potatoes with the maple syrup and sprinkle with the chili flakes. Add spoonfuls of yogurt, sour cream or crème fraîche, then dig in, with the lime wedges for squeezing.

4

Superfood Lentil Salad

Preparation time: 10 minutes
Cooking time: 5 minutes
Serves 4–6, easily doubled

Superfoods are rich in nutrients that do us good, and this salad is packed with them. I like to choose puy lentils for their firm texture and peppery, nutty taste, plus they look beautiful on the plate. If you can't find pre-cooked puy lentils, boil ½ cup (120 g) dried puy lentils in plenty of water for about 20 minutes, until just tender.

7 oz (200 g) broccolini
   (tenderstem broccoli)
3½ oz (100 g) snow peas
   (mangetouts)
1 lime
1 lemon
1 small piece of fresh ginger (enough
   to make ½ tsp grated)
1 fat clove garlic
½–1 tsp crushed chili flakes
   (optional)
1 tsp superfine (caster) sugar
1 tbsp sesame oil
½ red onion
½ cup (100 g) whole almonds
1½ cups (250 g) pre-cooked puy
   lentils
1 handful sprouts or cress (I use
   radish sprouts, which are available
   from my supermarket)
sea salt and freshly ground
   black pepper

1
Bring a pan of salted water to a boil. Cut the broccolini (tenderstem broccoli) into shorter lengths and chop the snow peas (mangetouts) in half, if you like.

2
Add the broccolini to the pan, let the water come back to a boil, then boil for 2 minutes. Add the snow peas and boil for another 1–2 minutes until the vegetables are just tender and very bright green.

Drain the vegetables, then submerge them in a bowl of cold water, changing the water several times to cool them quickly. This will help them to stay perky and green in the salad. Drain well and dab off excess water with paper towels.

3
Squeeze the lime and half the lemon, then pour the juice into a large bowl. Finely grate ½ tsp ginger and finely chop the garlic, then add to the bowl with the chili flakes, sugar, and sesame oil. Thinly slice the onion, add to the bowl and stir everything together.

4
Roughly chop the almonds.

5
Add the lentils and blanched vegetables to the dressing, then toss well. Season to taste with salt and pepper. Scatter the chopped almonds and sprouts over the salad, then serve.

Roasted Vegetable & Feta Couscous

Preparation time: 10 minutes,
plus cooling
Cooking time: 40 minutes
Serves 4–6 as a side, easily doubled

Rather than making this an overtly
Moroccan couscous salad, I've kept
things simple with a little lemon,
crunchy pecans, and a touch of
sweetness from dried cranberries,
so it will go with just about anything.
A great barbecue or picnic side and
lunchbox filler.

½ butternut squash

1 red onion

2 zucchini (courgettes)

2 bell peppers, ideally 1 red
    and 1 yellow

2 tbsp extra-virgin olive oil, plus
    more to dress if you like

¾ cup (80 g) pecan halves

1¾ cups (300 g) couscous

scant ½ cup (50 g) dried cranberries

1 organic (unwaxed) lemon

scant 2 cups (450 ml) just-boiled
    chicken or vegetable broth (stock)

1 bunch fresh flat-leaf parsley

3½ oz (100 g) feta cheese

sea salt and freshly ground
    black pepper

1
Preheat the oven to 400°F (200°C/ Gas Mark 6). Scoop the seeds from the squash with a spoon and discard. Cut the squash into bite-size cubes using a large, sharp knife. There's no need to peel the skin from the squash unless you really want to, as it will soften as it roasts.

2
Peel the onion and cut into chunky wedges. Slice the zucchini (courgettes) into thick rounds. Halve and deseed the bell peppers, then cut into chunky pieces. Put all of the vegetables into a large roasting pan, then drizzle with the olive oil and season well with salt and pepper.

3
Roast the vegetables for 20 minutes, turn them a few times in the oil, then add the pecans. Return to the oven for another 20 minutes.

4
While the vegetables cook, prepare the couscous. Put into a large bowl and stir in the cranberries. Finely grate in the lemon zest.

5
Pour the very hot broth (stock) over the top. Cover the bowl with plastic wrap (clingfilm) or a large plate to keep in the steam. Let the couscous stand for about 15 minutes, or longer if you have time.

6

When ready, the roasted vegetables should be tender and golden and the nuts will be toasted. Squeeze the juice of the lemon over the vegetables and let cool.

7

The couscous is ready when all of the broth has been absorbed. Fluff up the grains with a fork and let it cool a little. Toss with the vegetables and season to taste with salt and pepper. Roughly chop the parsley leaves and crumble the cheese.

8

Toss the parsley and feta through the salad just before serving, adding a drizzle more oil if it seems dry. It's best served just warm or at room temperature.

Spiced Carrot
& Herb Salad

Preparation time: 20 minutes,
plus cooling
Cooking time: 5 minutes

Carrots are rarely the star ingredient,
so this is a special salad to show
off all that's good about the humble
orange root. Cooked carrot salads
a little like this are common in
Moroccan and Portuguese cooking,
but in fact they go well with a
multitude of dishes from around
the world.

2¼ lb (1 kg) young or baby carrots
   (I used Chantenay)
2 cloves garlic
1 tsp fennel seeds
1 tsp coriander seeds
2 tsp cumin seeds
4 tbsp red wine vinegar
2 tbsp superfine (caster) sugar
4 tbsp extra-virgin olive oil, plus
   extra for drizzling
2 tbsp sesame seeds
1 bunch fresh mint
1 handful fresh dill
sea salt and freshly ground
   black pepper

1

Trim the tops from the carrots, then thinly slice lengthways. There's no need to peel them first. Thinly slice the garlic.

2

Put both the carrots and garlic into a large pan, cover with cold water and season with salt. Bring to a boil over high heat, then simmer for 5 minutes, or until the carrots are just tender.

3

Meanwhile, heat a skillet or frying pan, then add the fennel, coriander, and cumin seeds. Cook for a couple of minutes until the spices smell fragrant. Roughly crush the seeds in a mortar with a pestle.

4

Drain the carrots, then toss in a bowl with the toasted spices, vinegar, sugar, oil, and seasoning. While the carrots cool, they will absorb all of the flavors.

5

Wipe out the pan that you used for the spices, then add the sesame seeds. Cook the seeds for a few minutes, stirring often, until lightly golden.

6

When the salad has cooled, roughly chop the mint and dill leaves. Toss with the carrots and sesame seeds, then transfer to a serving dish. Drizzle with a little more oil if you like.

Fresh & Fluffy Flatbreads

Preparation time: 10 minutes, plus rising
Cooking time: 6 minutes
Serves 8, easily doubled

OK, you can buy perfectly good ready-made pita bread, but this is about having a bit of playtime in the kitchen. It's easier than you might think and actually a lot tastier. The breads go perfectly with the mezze on page 198, the lamb kofte on page 208, or any time you need some tasty bread for dipping and dunking. The milk-and-water mixture makes the dough extra soft in the middle.

3¾ cups (450 g) hard (strong) white
    bread flour, plus extra for
    rolling out
1 tsp or 1 x ¼-oz (7-g) package
    active dry (fast-action) yeast
2 tsp fine salt
⅔ cup (150 ml) milk, plus a little
    more for brushing
3 tbsp extra-virgin olive oil
1 tbsp sesame seeds
1 tbsp poppy seeds

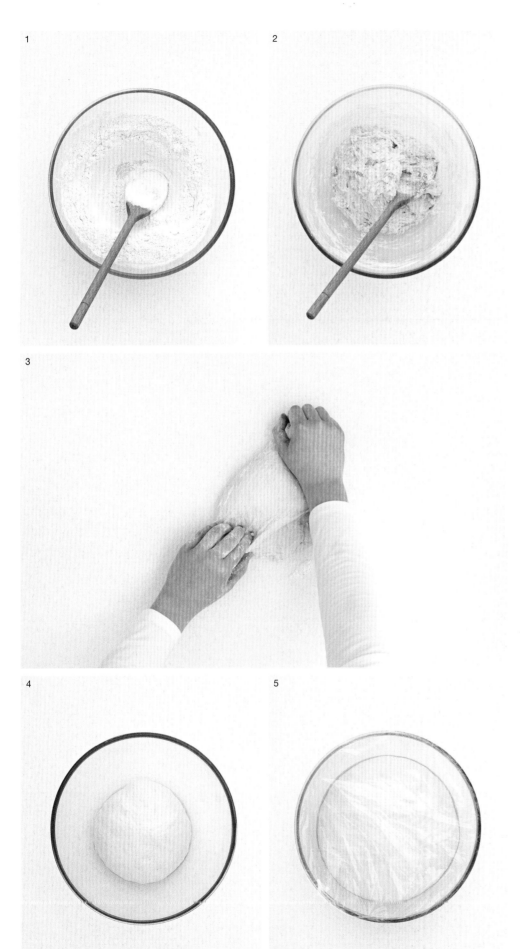

1

Put the flour into a large bowl, then add the yeast and salt and mix well. Make a well in the middle with a wooden spoon. Mix the milk, oil, and ⅔ cup (150 ml) just-warm water in a pitcher (jug).

2

Pour the liquid ingredients into the dry, then quickly mix together to make a rough dough. Try to avoid getting any overly wet or dry patches. Set aside for 10 minutes.

3

After 10 minutes, flour the work surface and your hands, then turn the dough out of the bowl. Knead it until smooth and springy, about 5 minutes. Add a little more flour if needed, but avoid adding too much, as it will dry the dough. As you work the dough it will become less and less sticky.

HOW TO KNEAD
As long as the dough is stretched and folded enough, it doesn't really matter how you do it. I hold the dough down with my left hand, then grab the dough at the far edge with my right and push it away to make the dough stretch. I then fold the stretched dough over itself, squash it down with my knuckles and turn it 90 degrees. Repeat until it is springy and bounces back when prodded.

4

When the dough is silky smooth and springy to the touch, stop kneading. Pour a little more oil into a large bowl, add the dough, then turn it over a few times until coated.

5

Cover the bowl with plastic wrap (clingfilm) then leave in a warm (not hot) place for about 1 hour, or until doubled in size.

If you want to make the dough the day before, let it rise in the fridge overnight. It will rise to the same size, only more slowly, and will have a richer flavor.

6
When the dough is ready, preheat the oven to 450°F (230°C/Gas Mark 8) and sprinkle 2 baking sheets with flour. Using a large knife dipped in flour, cut the dough into 8 pieces. Don't knead the dough before you roll it, as we want to retain any bubbles of air. It will also be easier to roll out. With extra flour on the rolling pin, roll the dough into a round or an oblong shape, until about ⅛ inch (3 mm) thick.

7
Lift the dough onto the prepared baking sheets. Using a pastry brush, brush the dough with a little milk, then sprinkle with the sesame or poppy seeds. The dough doesn't need to rise again.

8
Bake the breads for about 6 minutes, or until light and puffed and smelling delicious. To keep the breads soft, wrap in a clean dish towel while they are still hot, then let cool.

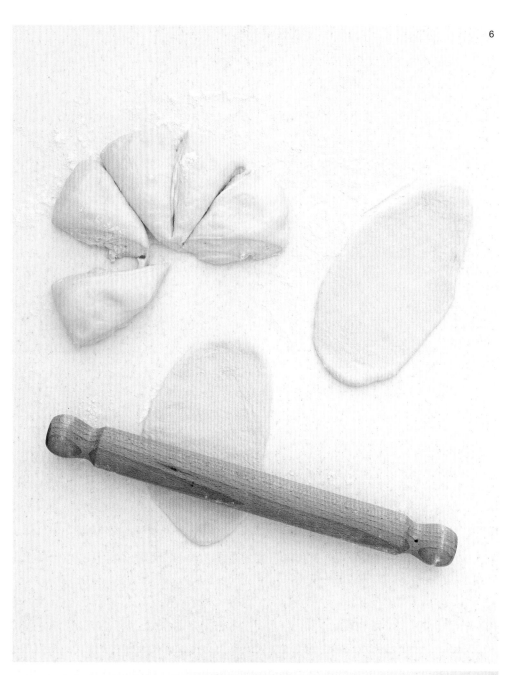

DESSERTS & BAKING

Summer Pudding Trifle

Preparation time: 20 minutes,
plus cooling and chilling
Cooking time: 10 minutes
Serves 8

This recipe takes all the best bits of summer pudding (lots of intense fruit) and a traditional trifle (rich vanilla custard, liquor, and billowing cream) to create a true taste of the season. The proportions of the berries can be varied: as long as you have 5 cups (900 g) of summer berries, plus 2¾ cups (300 g) ripe strawberries, things will turn out just fine.

2⅓ cups (400 g) raspberries

scant 2 cups (300 g) blackberries

scant 1 cup (100 g) red currants

scant 1 cup (100 g) black currants

generous ½ cup (120 g) superfine
   (caster) sugar, plus a little extra

2¾ cups (300 g) strawberries

4 eggs

2 tbsp cornstarch (corn flour)

1¼ cups (300 ml) whole milk

2½ cups (600 ml) heavy (double)
   cream

1 vanilla bean

7 oz (200 g) good-quality brioche
   or pound (Madeira) cake

5 tbsp orange liqueur
   (or orange juice for a
   non-alcoholic version)

1
Put three-quarters of the raspberries, blackberries and currants into a medium pan, then add scant ½ cup (80 g) of the sugar and 2 tablespoons water.

PREPARING CURRANTS
To remove currants from their stems, hold them over a bowl, then run a fork along the stem from top to bottom. The currants will come off easily.

2
Simmer for 2 minutes until the berries are surrounded with juice but mainly still intact. Remove the strawberry tops, then cut each strawberry in half or quarters if large. Stir most of the strawberries into the hot fruit, then let cool.

3
To make the custard, separate the eggs (see page 61) and put the yolks into a large bowl. Add the remaining sugar and the cornstarch (corn flour).

4
Whisk everything together until smooth.

5
Put the milk, 1¼ cups (300 ml) cream and half of the vanilla seeds into a medium pan, then bring just to a boil.

DESEEDING VANILLA BEANS
To scrape the vanilla seeds from the bean, slit the bean along its length, then run a small knife along each side.

6
Pour the hot liquid into the egg mixture, whisking constantly as you pour, until smooth and even

7

Return the custard to a clean pan, then bring to a boil over medium heat until thick and smooth, stirring all the time. Strain into a bowl, sprinkle the surface with a little sugar (this will stop a skin forming) and let cool for 15 minutes. Cover and transfer to the fridge to cool completely.

8

When the fruit and custard have cooled, it's time to layer up the trifle. Tear the brioche into pieces and put some into the bottom of a large serving bowl or trifle dish at least 3½ inches (9 cm) deep and 6-cup (1.5-litre) capacity. Sprinkle with some of the liqueur and let soak for a few seconds.

9

Spoon some of the fruit and its juice over the brioche, then layer the rest of the brioche and fruit until it has all been used up and the brioche is totally covered. Keep adding a little liqueur to the brioche as you go, saving 1 tablespoon for later.

10

Give the custard a quick whisk to make sure it's smooth, then spoon it on top of the fruit and spread to the edges. Chill the trifle for a few hours or overnight.

11

Whip the remaining cream with the rest of the vanilla and liqueur, until thickened but not stiff.

12

Spoon the cream over the trifle, then decorate with the reserved currants and berries.

Plum, Ginger, & Almond Tart

Preparation time: 40 minutes,
plus chilling
Cooking time: 50 minutes
Serves 8–12

With a rich frangipane filling and juicy fruit, this tart tastes every bit as good as something from the pâtisserie. It's a good recipe to start with if you're new to making pastry, as the method doesn't involve blind baking and the mixture is very forgiving. Switch the fruit as the seasons change—peaches, apricots, cherries, raspberries, and ripe pears would all work very well.

3 eggs

2 cups (225 g) all-purpose (plain)
   flour, plus 2 tbsp and extra for
   rolling out

½ tsp fine salt

1 stick (120 g) unsalted butter,
   very cold

¾ cup (150 g) plus 2 tbsp
   superfine (caster) sugar

6 ripe plums

7 tbsp (100 g) unsalted butter,
   softened

1¼ cups (150 g) ground almonds

½ tsp almond extract

½ tsp ground ginger

1 handful slivered (flaked) almonds

cream or ice cream, to
   serve (optional)

1

2

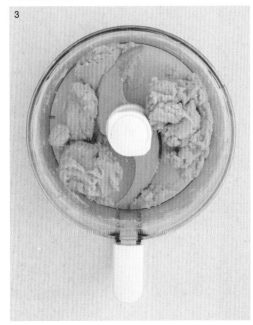

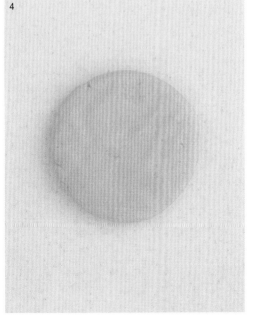

1
First, separate 1 egg (see page 61) and drop the yolk into a small bowl. Add 2 tablespoons cold water to the yolk, then beat together with a fork. Put 2 cups (225 g) flour into the bowl of a food processor and add ¼ teaspoon of the salt. Cut the cold butter into cubes, then scatter over the flour.

2
Process the butter and flour together for 5–10 seconds until the mixture resembles bread crumbs and no flecks of butter remain. Now pulse in the 2 tablespoons sugar.

3
Add the yolk mixture to the processor, then process in one-second bursts until a dough forms in big clumps.

LESS IS MORE
The key to tender, crumbly crust is not to overwork it and to keep it cool. If you don't have a food processor, rub the butter into the flour using your fingertips and thumbs until the mixture looks like fine bread crumbs. If the mixture starts to feel warm or the butter sticky, chill it for 5 minutes, then continue. Pour the eggs over the flour and butter mixture as evenly as you can, then use a round-bladed knife to mix to a dough.

4
Turn the dough onto the work surface and shape it into a flat disc. Wrap in plastic wrap (clingfilm) and chill for at least 30 minutes until firm, but not rock hard.

5
Dust the work surface and a rolling pin with flour. Have ready a 9-inch (23-cm) round, loose-bottom tart pan. Using a rolling pin, press shallow ridges evenly across the dough, then rotate it by a quarter turn. Repeat this until the pastry is about ½ inch (1 cm) thick. This will help the dough to stretch without becoming tough.

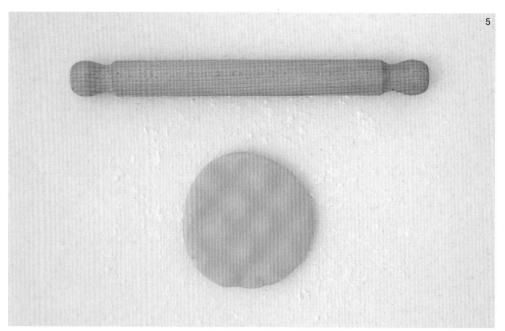

6
Now roll out the dough. Roll the rolling pin back and forth in one direction only, turning the dough by a quarter-turn every few rolls, until it's about ⅛ inch (3 mm) thick. Using a rolling pin to help, lift the dough over the pan.

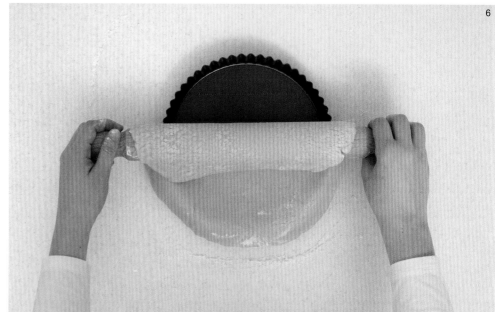

7
Ease the dough gently into the pan, allowing it to hang over the sides.

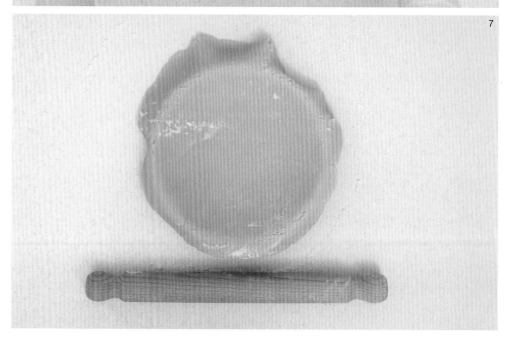

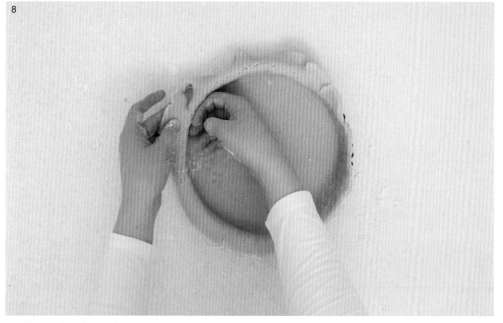

8
Gently persuade the dough into the side of the pan with the back of your fingers, lifting and supporting the overhanging dough with your other hand as you go.

9
Trim the top of the dough by rolling the rolling pin over the edge of the pan.

ANY HOLES?
If your dough has ripped or small holes have appeared, don't panic: it's common when making such a buttery crust. Dampen a little of the leftover dough and stick it down well to seal the gap.

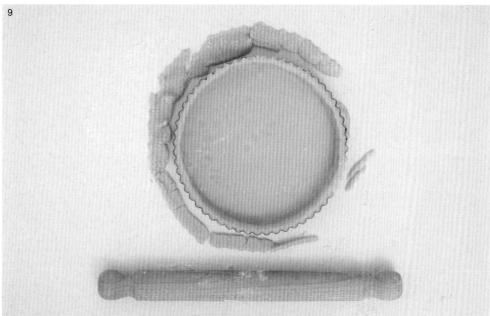

10
Prick the base several times with a fork. Now gently press the dough all around the sides of the pan, so that it rises above the rim by about ⅛ inch (3 mm). By doing this, your dough will still come to the top of the pan once it's baked, even if it shrinks a little. Chill in the fridge for 20 minutes or the freezer for 10 minutes until firm. Meanwhile, preheat the oven to 350°F (180°C/ Gas Mark 4). Set a rack in the middle of the oven, and put a baking sheet in to heat up.

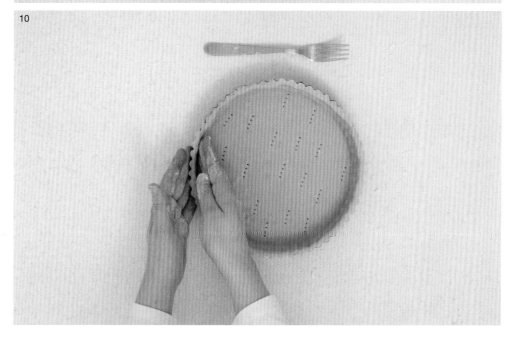

11

While you're waiting for the dough to chill, prepare the filling. Cut the plums in half and remove the pits (stones). Set aside. Put the remaining whole eggs, 2 tablespoons flour, ¼ teaspoon salt, ¾ cup (150 g) sugar, the soft butter, almonds, almond extract, and ground ginger, into a large bowl.

12

Beat the filling ingredients together until creamy and even-textured.

13

Spoon the filling into the crust, level the top, then arrange the plums over the top (don't press them in). Scatter the slivered (flaked) almonds around the fruit.

14

Slide the tart onto the hot baking sheet, then bake for 45–50 minutes until the filling is risen and golden all over and looks firm, and the plums are juicy and tender. Cool in the pan, then serve with cream, ice cream or thick cream with some chopped candied (preserved stem) ginger added.

BAKING TARTS
Baking the tarts on a hot baking sheet is a pastry-chef secret. The sheet acts as an even conductor of heat and helps the pastry to cook through underneath.

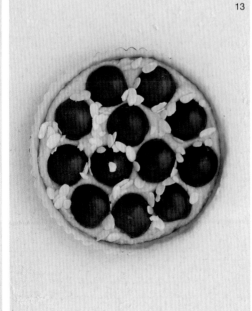

Strawberry Cream Cake

Preparation time: 20 minutes,
plus cooling
Cooking time: 25–30 minutes
Serves 10

This classic strawberry cream cake
has an almost all-in-one method,
which is quick to put together.
Sponge cakes are best enjoyed on
the day they are made, but a vanilla
syrup will help to keep them moist
for a day or two, stored in an
airtight container.

2 sticks (225 g) unsalted butter, very
    soft, plus extra for greasing
generous 1 cup (225 g) superfine
    (caster) sugar, plus 3 tbsp
4 eggs, at room temperature
2 tsp vanilla extract
¼ tsp fine salt
2 cups (225 g) all-purpose
    (plain) flour
2 tsp baking powder
1 tbsp milk, if needed
2¾ cups (300 g) strawberries
scant 1 cup (200 ml) whipping or
    heavy (double) cream
a little confectioners' (icing) sugar,
    to serve

1

Lightly butter two 8-inch (20-cm) shallow round cake pans, then line the bottoms with circles of parchment paper. Preheat the oven to 350°F (180°C/Gas Mark 4).

2

Put the butter and sugar into a large bowl, then beat with an electric mixer until creamy and very pale.

3

Add the eggs, 1 teaspoon vanilla and the salt to the bowl. Mix the flour and baking powder together, then sift on top.

4

Mix again briefly until even and smooth. It's important not to overwork the batter here, so stop as soon as everything is incorporated. If the mixture seems very stiff, add the milk and mix it in.

HOW FLOURS DIFFER

Depending on the kind of wheat used, the climate where you live, or even the brand you buy, flours can be drier or more damp, and this can affect your baking. This kind of cake batter should normally be soft enough to drop from the spoon, without being too stiff or too sloppy (although I've never found the latter to be a problem). Add the extra milk to your batter if you think it looks a bit on the thick side.

5

Use a spatula to scoop the batter evenly into the prepared cake pans, even out the tops, then bake in the middle of the oven for 25–30 minutes. If the cakes are browning unevenly, they can be swapped around in the oven safely after 25 minutes or when evenly risen and firm. Open the door any earlier and the cakes may sink.

6

While you wait, make the vanilla syrup. Put 2 tablespoons sugar and 2 tablespoons water in a small pan and heat very gently until the sugar dissolves. Remove from the heat, then add ½ teaspoon vanilla extract and let cool.

7

When ready, the cakes will be evenly risen through to the middle, evenly golden, and slightly shrunken away from the sides of the pans. To be sure, insert a skewer or toothpick into the middle of one of the cakes. If it comes out clean or with a few damp crumbs, it's ready. If it comes out with any uncooked mixture, return to the oven for 5 minutes more.

8

Let the cakes cool in their pans for 15 minutes, then remove from the pans, peel away the parchment paper and turn them onto a cooling rack, top side down and resting on the upturned parchment paper. This will stop the wires from making marks in the tops of the cakes. Poke the upturned cakes all over with a skewer or something similar, then spoon over the cooled syrup.

9

While you wait for the cakes to cool fully, roughly chop half of the strawberries. Thinly slice the rest.

10

Pour the cream into a large bowl and add the rest of the vanilla and the remaining 1 tablespoon sugar. Whip until thickened but not stiff.

11

Stir the chopped strawberries into the cream. Put 1 cake onto a serving plate, then spread with the strawberry cream.

12

Put the second cake on top, press it down a little, then top with the sliced strawberries. Dust with confectioners' (icing) sugar to serve.

Lime & Blackberry Polenta Cake

Preparation time: 15 minutes
Cooking time: about 50 minutes
Makes 12 slices

This is a beautiful Italian-style cake, made with polenta and almonds in lieu of flour, fragrant with lime and punctuated with tangy blackberries. Polenta is made from ground corn, and gives the cake its yellow glow. Look for quick-cooking polenta for this recipe, sometimes labelled fine cornmeal.

---

2 sticks (225 g) unsalted butter, very soft, plus extra for the pan

generous 1 cup (225 g) superfine (caster) sugar, plus 1 tbsp

1 lime

3 eggs, at room temperature

scant 1¼ cups (175 g) quick-cook polenta

2 cups (200 g) ground almonds

1½ tsp baking powder

¼ tsp fine salt

scant 2 cups (300 g) fresh (or thawed frozen) blackberries

light (single) cream, mascarpone cheese or thick yogurt, to serve

1

Preheat the oven to 325°F (160°C/ Gas Mark 3). Butter the inside of a 9-inch (23-cm) round springform cake pan, then use a circle of parchment paper to line the bottom.

2

Put the butter and sugar into a large bowl. Using an electric mixer, beat them together until creamy and pale.

3

Finely grate the lime zest, then add this to the bowl along with the eggs, polenta, almonds, baking powder, and salt.

4

Beat everything together until smooth and even and fairly thick. Fold in half of the berries, taking care not to crush them.

5

Pour the batter into the prepared tin and smooth the top. Bake the cake for 50 minutes, or until risen slightly and golden all over. Test if the cake is ready by inserting a skewer or toothpick (or even a strand of spaghetti) into the middle. The cake is ready if the skewer comes out dry with a few damp crumbs. If not, return it to the oven for 10 minutes more, then test it again.

6

Squeeze the juice from the lime, then mix with 1 tablespoon sugar. Let it dissolve as the cake bakes.

7

Let the cake cool in the pan until warm, then poke holes all over the cake with a skewer or toothpick and pour over the lime syrup. Let cool completely.

8

When the cake is totally cold, unclip the sides of the pan, carefully remove the bottom of the pan and lining paper, then put the cake onto a serving plate. Scatter the rest of the berries over the top. Serve with cream, mascarpone or thick yogurt.

Berry Crumble Ice Cream

Preparation time: 30 minutes,
plus freezing
Cooking time: 25 minutes
Serves 8–10

Condensed milk is the secret
ingredient here, creating a silky smooth
ice cream that doesn't need churning
in an ice-cream maker but tastes really
convincing. The basic vanilla mixture
would also be great with chocolate
chips, honeycomb, rum-soaked
raisins... whatever you like. Add them
at step 10 and freeze.

2½ cups (600 ml) heavy
    (double) cream
1 tsp vanilla extract
scant 1 cup (200 ml) condensed milk
scant 1 cup (100 g) all-purpose
    (plain) flour
1 pinch fine salt
4 tbsp (50 g) unsalted butter,
    very cold
4 tbsp superfine (caster) sugar
2¾ cups (300 g) mixed summer
    berries (fresh or frozen)

1

Pour the cream into a large mixing bowl, then add the vanilla. Using an electric mixer, whip the cream until thickened but not stiff.

2

Add the condensed milk to the cream, then use a spatula or large metal spoon to fold it in until evenly mixed. Try to conserve as much of the air in the cream as you can.

3

Put the mixture into a large freezer-proof container (I used a small 7 × 10-inch (18 × 25-cm) roasting pan—a baking dish would be fine too), cover with plastic wrap (clingfilm), then freeze for 3 hours, or until set but still spoonable.

4

Prepare the crumble topping and fruit while you wait. Preheat the oven to 350°F (180°C/Gas Mark 4). Mix the flour and salt together in a large bowl, then add the butter, cut into cubes.

5

Rub the butter into the flour, passing it through your fingers and thumbs until the cubes of butter start to be incorporated into the flour. If the mixture starts to feel warm or the butter sticky, chill it for 5 minutes, then continue. Keep rubbing your fingers together until the mixture looks like clumpy bread crumbs, then stir in 2 tablespoons of the sugar.

6

Spread out the crumble mixture over a large baking pan. Bake for about 25 minutes, until golden and crisp, taking a look halfway through. If the crumble is browning unevenly, break up with a spoon and stir it around a bit, then return to the oven. Let cool.

7

Put the fruit into a pan with the remaining 2 tablespoons sugar.

8

Heat gently until the fruit turns very soft and saucy, then let cool completely.

9

When the ice cream base is almost frozen but still spoonable, swirl in the fruit and its juice.

10

Sprinkle with the crumble, cover with plastic wrap (clingfilm), then freeze for at least another 4 hours, ideally overnight, or for up to 1 month. Take the ice cream out of the freezer 15 minutes before you want to serve it, to let it soften, ready for scooping.

Pistachio Yogurt Cake with Figs & Honey

Preparation time: 45 minutes
plus cooling
Cooking time: 45 minutes
Serves at least 8

I love the unique texture that yogurt gives to cakes and baked goods; sort of dense but light at the same time. Here I've mixed it with olive oil and pistachios to make a moist and tasty Middle-Eastern-style cake that's ideal for dessert with coffee or a glass of mint tea.

7 tbsp (100 g) unsalted butter,
  plus extra for greasing
scant ½ cup (100 ml) olive oil
3 eggs, at room temperature
scant 1 cup (200 g) Greek yogurt,
  plus extra to serve
1¾ cups (200 g) shelled pistachios
1¼ cups (150 g) all-purpose
  (plain) flour
2 tsp baking powder
¼ tsp fine salt
¾ cup (150 g) superfine
  (caster) sugar
6 fresh figs, or more if you like
2 tbsp honey, plus extra to serve

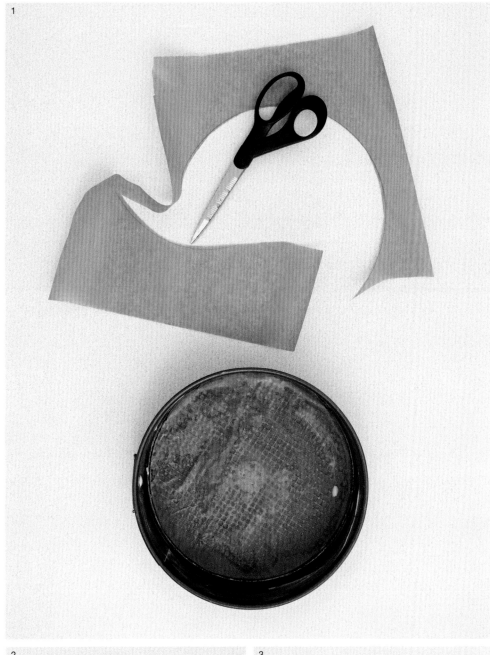

1
Butter the inside of a deep 8-inch (20-cm) round cake pan, then line the bottom with a circle of parchment paper. Preheat the oven to 325°F (160°C/Gas Mark 3).

2
Melt the butter in a pan, then pour it into a large mixing bowl. Pour in the oil and let cool for a few minutes.

3
Add the eggs and yogurt to the bowl and whisk until smooth and even.

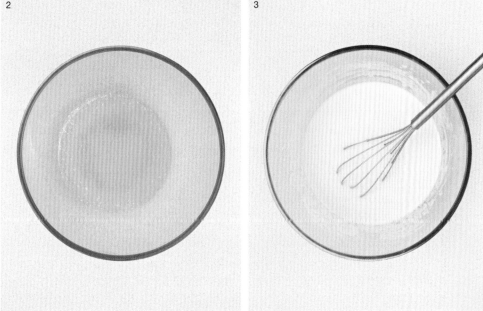

4

Put 1¼ cups (150 g) of the pistachios into a food processor with 1 tablespoon of the flour and process until fine and sandy. If you don't have a food processor, the next best thing is to put the pistachios into a food storage bag, squeeze out the air, then bash the nuts with a rolling pin until fine.

5

Add the nuts, flour, baking powder, salt and sugar to the buttery mixture, then fold together using a spatula or metal spoon until thoroughly combined. Pour the batter into the pan and even out the top.

6

Bake the cake for 45 minutes, or until evenly risen and golden and a skewer or toothpick inserted into the middle comes out clean. Cool the cake in its pan for 15 minutes, then transfer it to a cooling rack.

7

When ready to serve (it can be warm or cold, but is best warm), put the cake onto a serving plate. Slice the figs in half and sit a few pieces on top of the cake. Drizzle 2 tablespoons honey over the top of the cake and fruit, then sprinkle with the remaining whole nuts. Serve with the rest of the figs and more yogurt on the side. The cake will still be very good to eat a few days after baking.

CHOOSING FIGS
When buying figs, look for those that are dark and plump, and smell fragrant. Failing that, use fresh pomegranate seeds or fresh raspberries to scatter over the cake instead.

Strawberry Rhubarb Fool with Cinnamon Shortbread

Preparation time: 15 minutes,
plus chilling
Cooking time: 40 minutes
Serves 6–8

Early-season forced rhubarb is
the best choice if you can find it,
as the stalks are tender, sweeter,
and make brilliant, shocking pink
ripples through this creamy fool. To
make a quick version, you can mix
fresh strawberries with ready-made
rhubarb compote and cookies.

---

11 oz (300 g) rhubarb, pink if
   possible, choose thinner stalks

¾ cup (150 g) superfine (caster)
   sugar, plus extra for sprinkling

1 orange

2¼ cups (250 g) strawberries,
   at room temperature

7 tbsp (100 g) unsalted butter,
   softened

1 cup (120 g) all-purpose (plain) flour

4 tbsp rice flour or ground rice
   (if you can't find this, use
   extra all-purpose (plain) flour)

1 tsp ground cinnamon

1 pinch of salt

1¼ cups (300 ml) heavy (double)
   cream

scant 1 cup (200 g) fromage blanc
   (fromage frais) or low-fat
   Greek yogurt

1

Preheat the oven to 400°F (200°C/ Gas Mark 6). Cut the rhubarb into short lengths, put into a large baking dish, then sprinkle with scant ½ cup (80 g) of the sugar and toss well. Finely grate the zest from the orange, squeeze half the juice and sprinkle both over the rhubarb. Arrange the rhubarb in a single layer, then bake for 15–20 minutes, or until soft and syrupy.

2

While you wait, cut the strawberries into halves, or quarters if very large. Toss the berries with the hot rhubarb and its syrup, then let cool. The syrup will soften the strawberries.

3

For the shortbread, put the butter and remaining sugar into a large bowl and beat together until creamy.

4

Sift together the flour, ground rice, cinnamon and salt, then fold into the butter mixture. Try not to overwork the mixture, as this can make the shortbread tough.

5

Shape the dough into a cylinder about 2¾ inches (7 cm) across, then wrap in plastic wrap (clingfilm) and chill or freeze until firm, but not solid. This dough can be kept in the freezer for up to a month, if you like.

6

Turn the oven down to 350°F (180°C/Gas Mark 4). Cut the shortbread dough into 12 rounds about ½ inch (1 cm) thick using a serrated knife. Spread them out on a nonstick baking sheet.

7

Bake the cookies for 15–20 minutes, or until golden. Sprinkle with a little sugar, then cool on the sheet until firm. Transfer to a rack to cool completely.

8

When ready to serve, whip the cream and fromage blanc (fromage frais) or yogurt together until thickened but not stiff, then fold in the cooled rhubarb and strawberry mixture. If the fruit has released lots of juice, then hold some back, as it will make the fool too soft.

9

Spoon the fool into glasses or bowls and serve with a couple of shortbread on the side.

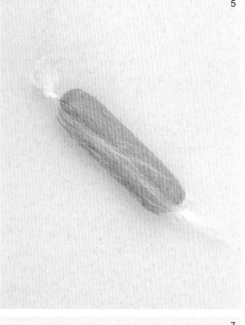

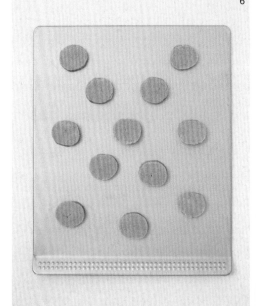

Melba Sundaes

Preparation time: 10 minutes
Serves 4, easily doubled or halved

The combination of raspberry sauce, peaches, and vanilla ice cream makes a delicious sundae that everyone will love. I've suggested using nectarines, as fuzzy peach skin spoils the texture for me, but choose whatever you like, looks best and smells most fragrant at the market. Adults might like a little splash of amaretto liqueur over the top of the ice cream.

1 quart (1 litre) vanilla ice cream

1¼ cups (200 g) raspberries

2 tbsp confectioners' (icing) sugar, or to taste

4 ripe nectarines or peaches

12 crisp amaretti cookies

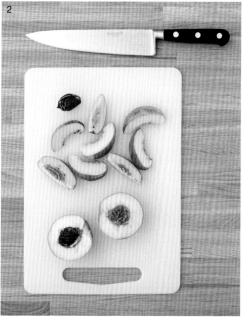

1

Take the ice cream from the freezer 10 minutes before you need to scoop it. Using either a hand-held blender or a food processor, process the raspberries and confectioners' (icing) sugar together to make a coulis. Taste and add more sugar if you like, although remember that the ice cream will be fairly sweet. There's no need to worry about straining out the seeds.

2

Halve the nectarines, then remove the pits (stones). Slice each half into 4 wedges.

3

Crush the amaretti very coarsely. To serve the sundaes, have ready 4 large sundae dishes or tumblers. Start with a scoop of ice cream, a few pieces of nectarine, then a drizzle of raspberry sauce and sprinkling of amaretti crumbs. Repeat the layers until the glasses are full to overflowing, then serve immediately.

Scones with Raspberry Crush Cream

Preparation time: 10 minutes
Cooking time: 15–20 minutes
Makes 8–10

No classic afternoon tea would be complete without a pile of scones, crusty outside and topped with cream. I've shaped my scones into big triangles so you won't need a special cutter. Make them on the day they're going to be eaten—they only take 30 minutes from start to finish, after all.

6 tbsp (80 g) unsalted butter,
    very cold
3 cups (350 g) all-purpose (plain)
    flour, plus extra for dusting
1 tbsp baking powder
¼ tsp fine salt
5 tbsp superfine (caster) sugar
1 egg
⅔ cup (150 ml) whole milk
1¼ cup (200 g) raspberries
¾ cup (200 g) extra-thick cream,
    crème fraîche, clotted cream,
    or heavy (double) cream

1
Preheat the oven to 425°F (220°C/ Gas Mark 7). Put a baking sheet in the top third of the oven to heat up. Cut the butter into cubes. Put the flour, baking powder, and salt into a large bowl and mix well. Add the butter.

2
Rub the butter into the flour mixture using your fingertips until the mixture looks like bread crumbs. If you have a food processor, then simply process the butter into the dry ingredients until fine. Stir in the sugar.

3
Beat the egg with a fork. Add 2 tablespoons of egg to the milk, then add to the dry ingredients.

4
Working quickly, mix the wet and dry ingredients together to make a soft, rough dough.

5

Flour your hands and the work surface thoroughly. Using your hand, bring the dough together to one big clump. Turn it onto the work surface. Knead the dough a couple of times just to smooth it a little (it's essential for fluffy scones that you don't overwork it at this point), then shape it into a log about 12 inches (30 cm) long. Cut the dough into equal triangles, dipping your knife into some flour each time to prevent the blade from sticking.

6

Brush the scones lightly with some of the remaining egg and then sprinkle with the rest of the sugar. This will make a crunchy golden crust as the scones bake. Remove the baking sheet from the oven, sprinkle a little flour over it, then lift the scones onto it, using something flat like a spatula (fish slice) to help. The heat from the hot tray will give the scones a head start and help them to grow tall and fluffy.

7

Bake the scones for 15 minutes or until they are golden and risen, and sound hollow when tapped underneath. Cool the scones on a rack. Crush the raspberries, then fold them into the cream or crème fraîche to serve. If using heavy (double) cream, whip it until thick but not stiff, adding a little confectioners' (icing) sugar to taste if you like, then stir in the berries.

Mango & Black Currant Sorbet

Preparation time: 30 minutes, plus freezing
Cooking time: 5 minutes
Serves 6–8

This gorgeous sorbet will brighten the end of any meal. When choosing mangoes, pick those that are ripe but not too ripe, with just a slight yield when pressed. You could turn the mixture into sorbet lollies if you have a set of molds—fill them at step 8, then freeze.

1½ cups (300 g) white superfine (caster) sugar
3–4 large, just-ripe mangoes, about 3¼ lb (1.5 kg) in total
3 large, or 4–5 smaller limes
3½ oz (100 g) fresh (or thawed frozen) black currants
1 large (UK medium) egg (optional)

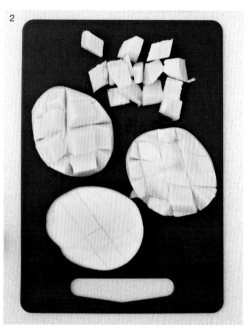

1

Put generous 1 cup (225 g) of the sugar into a medium pan, then pour in 1 cup (250 ml) cold water. Put the pan over a gentle heat and stir every now and again until the sugar has dissolved. When it has dissolved, and not before, boil the mixture for 1 minute, then let cool while you cut up the mango.

2

Cut the sections of the mango away from the pit (stone) in the middle, then cut away any flesh from around the middle too. Cut deep criss-crossed cuts into the sections, stopping when you get to the skin, then push the flesh inside out so it looks like a hedgehog. Cut away the flesh.

3

Squeeze the juice from the limes— you will need scant ½ cup (100 ml). Put the lime juice and mango chunks into a food processor, then process until smooth. Add the cooled syrup and process again.

4

Line a 2-quart (2-litre) freezer proof container with a large sheet of plastic wrap (clingfilm) (a little oil will help it stick to the sides of the container, if it's being tricky), then pour in the sorbet mixture. Put into the freezer and leave until solid, or almost there. This will take about 6 hours, or overnight is best.

5

Make the black currant ripple while you wait. Put the currants into a pan, then add the remaining sugar and 1 tablespoon water. Cook gently until the fruit is very soft. Strain the currant sauce through a fine-mesh strainer and leave it to cool. Discard what's left in the strainer (sieve).

6

When the mango mixture is firm, turn it out of the container and cut it into pieces.

7

Put the pieces into the bowl of the processor and pulse until smooth and thick. You might need to wait a few minutes for the mixture to soften a little if it's frozen really hard. If you want to use the egg white, separate the egg and add it now.

WHY AN EGG WHITE?
Adding an egg white to the final mixture gives the finished sorbet a smoother, more silky texture, and most sorbets are made this way. If you are concerned about serving a dish containing uncooked whites, then just leave the egg out. Alternatively, you can buy pasteurized whites from some supermarkets, which are worry-free.

8

Give the black currant sauce a quick stir, as it tends to set a little like jam as it cools. Spoon half of the mango mixture back into the freezer container, then swirl half of the black currant sauce over it. Repeat, then cover and freeze the sorbet for another 6 hours or until firm again. The sorbet will keep for up to 1 month.

9

Remove the sorbet from the freezer 10 minutes before you want to eat it, then scoop and serve in small bowls or ice cream cones.

Muscat & Honey Poached Peaches

Preparation time: 15 minutes,
plus cooling
Cooking time: 15 minutes
Serves 6

Glowing gold and scented with
vanilla and wine, these peaches
are heavenly by themselves and
low fat too. Should your halo slip,
add a spoonful of thick cream or
mascarpone to the side of your plate
for one of the best summer desserts
there is.

---

1 organic (unwaxed) lemon

1 vanilla bean

1 cinnamon stick

generous 1½ cups (375 ml) sweet
    Muscat dessert wine, or full and
    fruity white wine, such as
    Chardonnay or Viognier if you
    can't find it

3 tbsp honey, such as
    orange flower honey

½ cup (100 g) superfine (caster)
    sugar

6 ripe peaches

thick heavy (double) cream or
    mascarpone cheese, to serve
    (optional)

1
Pare the zest from the lemon using a vegetable peeler and split the vanilla bean down the middle.

2
Choose a pan that's big enough to hold the peaches in a single layer. Put the zest, vanilla, cinnamon stick, wine, honey and sugar into the pan, then add 1¼ cups (300 ml) water. Heat gently until the honey and sugar have dissolved. Bring the liquid to a simmer, then add the peaches to the pan (the liquid might not completely cover them, but that's OK).

3
Cover the peaches with a large scrunched-up circle of parchment paper. This will help to keep them submerged in the syrup.

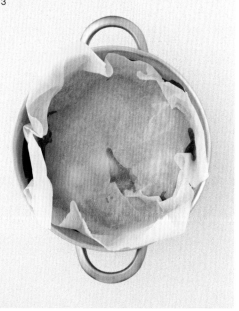

4

Cook the peaches for about
15 minutes in total, or until softened
but not mushy, lifting the paper
and turning them over very gently
four times so that they cook evenly.

5

Lift the peaches out of the syrup,
then leave until cool enough to
handle. Remove the vanilla bean,
cinnamon stick, and lemon zest too.
Boil the syrup for 5 minutes to
concentrate the flavors. Let it cool.

6

Slip the skins from the cooled
peaches. I find this easiest if I make
a little nick in the skin at the base of
the peach, then ease the skin away
carefully with my finger and thumb.
Discard the skins.

7

Pour the cooled syrup over the
peaches, then either chill until ready
to eat, or serve. I think they are the
most delicious at room temperature.
Serve with cream or mascarpone if
you like.

Raspberry & Passion Fruit Mallow Meringue

Preparation time: 30 minutes
plus cooling
Cooking time: 1 hour
Serves 8 generously

Crisp on the outside, light and soft within, this crowd-pleaser is easier to make than you may think. Rather than topping the meringue base with an overly rich topping, I like to use a mixture of cream and yogurt, and crown it with juicy fruit.

5 eggs

¾ cup (150 g) superfine (caster) sugar

1¼ cups (150 g) confectioners' (icing) sugar, plus 1–2 tbsp for the topping

1 tsp cornstarch (corn flour)

1¼ cups (300 ml) heavy (double) cream

1¼ cups (300 g) Greek yogurt

1 tsp vanilla extract

1½ cups (250 g) raspberries

4 large, ripe, wrinkly passion fruit

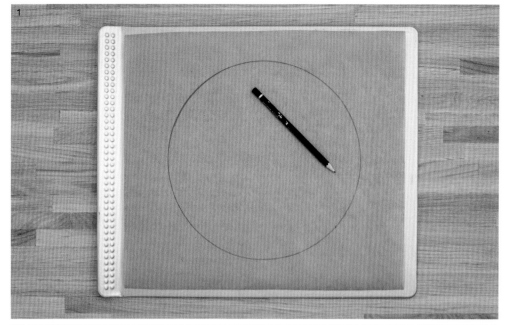

1

Use a pencil to mark a circle about 10 inches (25 cm) in diameter on a piece of parchment paper. A large dinner plate is about the right size to use as a template. Use this to line a large baking sheet or tray, remembering to turn the paper over or you'll end up with a pencil mark on your meringue. Preheat the oven to 300°F (150°C/Gas Mark 2) and set a shelf in the middle of the oven.

2

Separate the eggs and put the whites into a large and spotlessly clean glass or metal bowl.

SEPARATING AN EGG

Gently crack the shell against the side of a small bowl. Slowly pull the shell apart as cleanly as possible along the crack, tipping the yolk into one half of the shell. Let the white drain away into a bowl below. Drop the yolk into another small bowl. Separate the next egg over a third bowl—that way if you accidentally break the yolk, it won't contaminate the clean whites.

FAT-FREE

Grease is the enemy of egg whites and if any does end up in the bowl, the whites will not foam. I like to wipe the bowl with a piece of paper towel dampened with vinegar or lemon juice before adding the whites. Never use a plastic bowl, as grease can hide in scratches in the surface, even if the bowl looks clean.

3

Using an electric mixer, whisk the egg whites until the beaters leave a stiff peak when you pull them away from the bowl. Take care not to overwhisk the whites at this stage.

4

This photograph shows overwhisked egg whites, which look dry and cottony at the edges, and slightly separated and watery at the bottom of the bowl. Overwhisking the whites at this stage makes it hard to get a good result later on.

5

Add 1 tablespoon of the superfine (caster) sugar, then whisk the mixture back to stiff peaks. Keep adding and whisking the superfine sugar, one spoon at a time. The meringue will start turning from fluffy to thick, and will have a pearly sheen.

When all of the superfine sugar has been added, the meringue will look thick and very pearlescent, rather like shaving foam.

6

Sift in 1¼ cups (150 g) confectioners' (icing) sugar and the cornstarch (corn flour), then fold them into the mixture using a large metal spoon.

FOLDING
Don't undo all your hard work with the whisk at this point. Cut the confectioners' sugar into the whites, then fold in a figure-eight motion, keeping a light touch to conserve the air bubbles. Stirring the meringue will cause it to lose volume.

7

Spoon the meringue onto the paper, then spread it out to fit within the circle. Create a rough nest shape, with a shallow indentation in the middle.

8

Bake the meringue for 30 minutes, then turn the temperature down to 275°F (140°C/Gas Mark 1) and bake for another 30 minutes until the pavlova is crisp on the outside and has taken on the palest hint of gold. Leave in the oven until cold. In an ideal world, make the meringue the evening before you need it and leave it in the oven overnight. A few small cracks are to be expected, but cooling it slowly will prevent any major crevasses appearing.

9

To make the topping, whip together the cream, yogurt, vanilla extract and remaining confectioners' sugar until thick but not stiff. Cut the passion fruit in half and scoop out the pulp.

CHOOSING PASSION FRUIT
As they ripen, passion fruit become more wrinkly, and the pulp inside the hard shell becomes sweeter and more perfumed. Avoid any that look too shrivelled, and pick those heavy for their size and with a purple-yellow hue.

10

Swirl the creamy mixture over the top of the meringue, then sprinkle with the raspberries and drizzle with the passion fruit seeds.

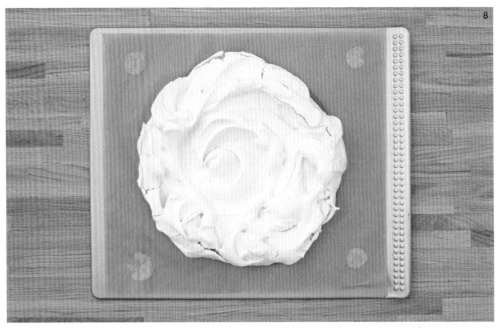

Chocolate Mousse with Cherries

Preparation time: 20 minutes, plus chilling
Makes 6 large or 8 smaller portions

What better excuse to eat chocolate mousse than the arrival of the cherry season? The slightly retro combination is well worth revisiting—good chocolate and a splash of kirsch (clear brandy made with cherries) will really make the fruit taste pop.

---

5 oz (150 g) semisweet (dark) chocolate, 70% cocoa

1½ cups (350 ml) heavy (double) cream

2 eggs, at room temperature

1 tbsp kirsch, brandy or water

4 tbsp superfine (caster) sugar

12 oz (350 g) ripe cherries

1 lemon

1
Chop the chocolate into small pieces, then put into a large heatproof bowl. Pour ¾ cup (150 ml) of the cream into a small pan, then bring just to a boil.

2
When the cream has bubbles appearing at the sides and the surface is shimmering, it's ready. Pour the hot cream onto the chocolate and let melt for about 3 minutes.

3
While you wait, separate the eggs (see page 321), and put the whites into a clean, grease-free bowl. Beat the yolks with the kirsch, brandy or water. Stir the now-melted chocolate and cream together until throughly blended, then add the yolk mixture and 2 tablespoons of the sugar. Stir until smooth and blended.

4
Pour another ¾ cup (150 ml) cream into a bowl. Using an electric hand mixer, first beat the egg whites until thick and foamy, but not stiff. Then whisk the cream until thick but not stiff. Do it this way around and you won't need to wash the beaters in between (cream on the beaters would prevent the whites from whipping).

5
Fold the cream into the chocolate mixture using a large metal spoon or a rubber spatula.

6

Now add a quarter of the whites and stir them in. This will loosen the mixture and get it ready for the rest of the whites. Spoon in the remainder, then fold in gently until the mixture is thoroughly blended, with no traces of white.

FOLDING
Using a figure-eight motion, cut and fold rather than stir the egg whites into the creamy chocolate mix. Try to conserve as much air as you can.

7

Spoon the mousse into 6 large or 8 small serving glasses or cups and chill for at least 2 hours or until firm.

8

To prepare the cherries, first cut them in half and remove the pits (stones).

9

Put the cherries into a skillet or frying pan with the remaining sugar and 2 teaspoons lemon juice. Cook the cherries over high heat for 1 minute or so, until the sugar melts and bubbles around the cherries. Let cool.

10

Whip the remaining cream, then spoon it on top of the mousses. Serve with the cherries.

TRY THIS
For cute little Black Forest gateaux pots, why not layer the cherries, mousse, and some ready-made chocolate cake in glasses, then top with whipped cream and a few more cherries.

Lemon Meringue
Ice Cream

Preparation time: 20 minutes,
plus cooling and freezing
Cooking time: 10 minutes
Serves 6

This is based on a recipe from Leith's
School of Food and Wine in London,
where I trained many moons ago.
Their clever recipe blends homemade
lemon curd with thick yogurt to make
a very easy ice cream. I've added a
bit more curd and crunch to create a
frilly and fabulous sort of semifreddo.

3 organic (unwaxed) lemons

6 eggs

1 stick plus 2 tbsp (150 g) unsalted
    butter

scant 1 cup (175 g) superfine
    (caster) sugar

2 oz (50 g) ready-made meringues

2 cups (500 g) Greek or thick,
    plain yogurt

1

Lightly oil the inside of a 1-quart (1-litre) loaf pan, then line it with a sheet of plastic wrap (clingfilm). If you don't have a loaf pan, then just use a medium baking dish or something similar. Finely grate the zest from the lemons and set aside. Squeeze the juice into a medium pan. Separate the eggs, then put the yolks into the pan with the butter and the sugar.

SEPARATING AN EGG
Gently crack the shell against the side of a small bowl. Slowly pull the shell apart as cleanly as possible along the crack, tipping the yolk into one half of the shell. Let the white drain away into a bowl below. Drop the yolk into another small bowl. Separate the next egg over a third bowl—that way if you accidentally break the yolk, it won't contaminate the clean whites. See page 321 for a photograph.

2

Place the pan over very low heat, then stir until the butter has melted and everything is evenly mixed. Keep cooking the mixture until it thickens enough to coat the back of the wooden spoon. Don't let the mixture boil, as the eggs will curdle.

3

Strain the lemon curd through a strainer (sieve) into a bowl, then add the lemon zest. Spoon 4 tablespoons of the curd into the bottom of the pan and spread it out evenly. Let cool.

4

Roughly break up the meringues with your fingers.

5

When the lemon curd is cold, add the yogurt to the bowl and mix until throughly blended.

6

Fold half of the meringues into the ice-cream mixture and spoon into the pan. Freeze for at least 6 hours or ideally overnight, until solid. The meringues will mostly melt into the ice cream as it freezes, adding pockets of meringue flavor here and there. The ice cream can be made up to 2 weeks ahead of time.

7

Transfer the ice cream to the fridge 10 minutes before serving so that it can soften enough to slice. Invert the pan over a serving plate and give it a tap to loosen. Remove the plastic wrap, then sprinkle with the rest of the meringue pieces. Slice and serve. I find dipping my knife in hot water before slicing helps to keep things neat and tidy.

White Chocolate
& Blueberry Cheesecake

Preparation time: 25 minutes,
plus chilling
Cooking time: 5 minutes
Serves 8

Super-smooth, creamy and no need
to bake, this is an mmm-inducing
treat for cheesecake lovers, which
in my experience is most people! The
white chocolate base goes beautifully
with any summer fruit or even
shavings of contrasting semisweet
(dark) chocolate.

7 oz (200 g) white chocolate

5 oz (150 g) graham crackers
   (digestive biscuits)

6 tbsp (80 g) unsalted butter

1 tbsp superfine (caster) sugar

1¼ cups (300 g) cream cheese, at
   room temperature

1 cup (250 g) mascarpone cheese,
   at room temperature

11 oz (300 g) blueberries

1

3

1

Bring a pan of water to a gentle simmer. Break the chocolate into chunks and put into a heatproof bowl. Put the bowl on top of the pan (it's very important that the bottom of the bowl doesn't touch the water). Let melt for about 5 minutes, stirring a couple of times. To keep the chocolate from burning, I tend to take the bowl from the heat while there are a few small lumps remaining, and let them melt in the heat of the surrounding chocolate.

MELTING CHOCOLATE
IN THE MICROWAVE
If you have a microwave, put the cubes into a large nonmetallic bowl and heat on low power for 1½ minutes, stirring halfway through.

2

While the chocolate is melting, make the base. Grease the inside of a 12 × 8-inch (30 × 20-cm) shallow baking pan and line it with parchment paper. Put the graham crackers (digestive biscuits) into a large food storage bag, then bash them with a rolling pin until completely crushed.

3

Melt the butter in a pan, add the crumbs and stir well to coat. Spoon the crumbs into the bottom of the pan, then press to even them out using the back of the spoon.

4

When the chocolate has melted, add the cream cheese and mascarpone to the bowl and whisk together until smooth and creamy. Spoon on top of the crumb base, then chill in the fridge for at least 4 hours, or until firm. The cheesecake can be made up to 2 days ahead if you like, or can even be frozen for up to a week, then thawed in the fridge.

5

For the topping, put the blueberries and the sugar into a medium pan. Cook over medium heat for about 5 minutes, until the berries are soft and surrounded with syrup. Set aside to cool.

6

Slice the cheesecake into squares or rectangles. Spoon the berry sauce around and over each piece just before serving.

END MATTERS

Planning a Menu

Whatever the occasion I'm cooking for, I like to spend a few quiet minutes planning my menu. Nothing complicated, just checking that what I have in mind will go together as a meal and working out what will be cooked and when.

When it comes to what to serve with what, balance is the key word. Avoid repeating similar tastes, textures, and ingredients, and remember we eat with our eyes, so appearance is important too. Many recipes in *Fresh & Easy* come with a side dish built in so you don't have to worry about matching a side with the main course.

As with my first book, *What to Cook and How to Cook It*, the recipes in this book were conceived as stand-alone favorites, although many of them can work together as tasty meals. The menus can be easily multiplied up or down to suit your needs. Feel free to pick and choose as you like; but if you're feeding only a handful of people and want to make one of the larger desserts, then I'd recommend leaving quantities as they are and enjoying the leftovers over the next few days.

For picnics and barbecues, a few well-prepared choices will keep serving simple and everyone happy. Why not ask friends to bring a dish, or cheat a little with a few treats from the deli counter?

Pick two of the courses from each menu to keep things simple, or three if you have a bit more time. If you like the sound of one menu, but don't have the right number of people, then adjust the quantities up and down. I have given most attention to main meals, plus a few ideas for barbecues, picnics, and other big summer events.

Romantic dinner
Asparagus & Poached Egg with Balsamic Butter (page 72)
Spicy Shrimp (Prawn), Fennel, & Chile Linguine (page 68)
Chocolate Mousse with Cherries (page 326)

Lunch al fresco
Spicy Shrimp (Prawn), Fennel, & Chile Linguine (page 68)
Steak & Artichoke Tagliata (page 158)
Berry Crumble Ice Cream (page 294)

Midweek suppers
Chicken & Ham Parmesan (page 84)
Melba Sundaes (page 306)

Grilled Halloumi with Pomegranate Tabbouleh (page 56)
Carrot Falafel with Sesame Sauce (page 64)
Zingy Fruit Salad (page 44)

Peach & Mozzarella Platter (page 82)
Seared Tuna with Sauce Vierge (page 154)
Lime & Blackberry Polenta Cake (page 290)

Summer dinner parties
Easy Mezze (page 198)
Lamb Kofte with Tzatziki (page 208)
Pistachio Yogurt Cake with Figs & Honey (page 298)

Lemon & Basil Gnudi (page 168)
Herb-Crusted Lamb with Pea Puree & Tomatoes (page 146)
Strawberry Rhubarb Fool with Cinnamon Shortbread (page 302)

Shrimp (Prawn) & Asparagus Skewers (page 220)
Lemon-Roasted Fish & Slow-Cooked Beans (page 194)
Muscat & Honey Poached Peaches (page 316)

Family barbecues

Sticky BBQ Chicken & Slaw (page 204)
Roasted Vegetable & Feta
	Couscous (page 260)
Pasta Salad with Tomato Pesto
	(page 106)

Sticky Soy Ribs with Asian Slaw
	(page 224)
Chicken & Blue Cheese Waldorf Salad
	(page 76)
Potato, Bacon, & Watercress Salad
	(page 250)

Chimichurri-Style Burgers (page 228)
Hasselback Sweet Potatoes
	(page 256)
Sweet Corn with Cheesy Butter
	(page 252)

Smart barbecues

Spinach & Ricotta Pastries with Sweet
	Bell Pepper Dip (page 136)
Lamb Kofte with Tzatziki (page 208)
Spicy Mackerel with Orange &
	Radish Salad (page 216)
Grilled Halloumi with Pomegranate
	Tabbouleh (page 56)

Peach & Mozzarella Platter (page 82)
Lemon & Herb Pork with Fennel
	& Mint Salad (page 212)
Goat Cheese & Polenta Stacks
	(page 232)

Independence Day celebration

Hot Dogs with Tomato, Sage, &
	Onion Relish (page 236)
Sticky BBQ Chicken & Slaw (page 204)
Green Salad with Seeds & Croutons
	(page 248)
Hasselback Sweet Potatoes (page 256)
Sweet Corn with Cheesy Butter
	(page 252)
Potato, Bacon, & Watercress Salad
	(page 250)
White Chocolate & Blueberry
	Cheesecake (page 334)
Raspberry & Passion Fruit Mallow
	Meringue (page 320)

Help-yourself family buffet

Roasted Summer Vegetable Lasagna
	(page 186)
Cobb Salad with Honey Mustard
	Dressing (page 140)
Roasted Vegetable & Feta Couscous
	(page 260)
Green Salad with Seeds &
	Croutons (page 248)
Raspberry & Passion Fruit Mallow
	Meringue (page 320)

Middle Eastern feast

Easy Mezze (page 198)
Fragrant Chicken with Quinoa Salad
	(page 190)
Spiced Carrot & Herb Salad
	(page 264)
Fattoush Salad with Labneh
	(page 110)
Pistachio Yogurt Cake with Figs &
	Honey (page 298)

Flavors of Asia

Sticky Soy Ribs with Asian Slaw
	(page 224)
Crisp Duck & Pineapple Salad
	(page 162)
Vietnamese Herb & Noodle Salad
	(page 88)
Superfood Lentil Salad (page 258)
Zingy Fruit Salad (page 44)

Cinco de mayo

Pulled Pork Sharing Plate (page 182)
Chimichurri-Style Burgers (page 228)
Mango & Black Currant Sorbet
	(page 312)

Family picnic

Spicy Chicken with Mango Raita
	(page 128)
Cobb Salad with Honey Mustard
	Dressing (page 140)
Ham, Mustard, & Fava (Broad) Bean
	Tart (page 118)
Roasted Vegetable & Feta Couscous
	(page 260)
Blueberry & Cream Cheese Muffins
	(page 36)

Nibbles with drinks

Many of my recipes can be served in buffet-sized portions, with just a few small adaptations:

Avocado & Chorizo Toast (page 28): Top small pieces of toast with avocado, chorizo and the cilantro (coriander).

Breakfast Blinis with Smoked Salmon (page 40): Make small blinis, spread the cheese mix over them, then top with a slice of salmon.

Lamb Kofte with Tzatziki (page 208): Make mini meatballs, then serve with mini pita bread and tzatziki.

Carrot Falafel (page 64): Serve falafel on a platter with a bowl of sesame sauce.

Chimichurri-style Burgers (page 228): Make sliders by pan-frying small patties of the burger mixture and serve in small buns with the salsa.

Chicken & Blue Cheese Waldorf (page 76): Serve the salad in small lettuce leaf boats (such as Little Gem or Belgian endive), topped with a slice of chicken.

Shrimp (Prawn) and Asparagus Skewers (page 220): Cook the shrimp (prawns) and asparagus on a grill pan (griddle), without skewers, then serve with the Mint Aïoli as a dip.

Tomato Pissaladière Tarts (page 124): Cut small circles of pastry, top with onion, one slice of tomato and remaining ingredients.

Chocolate Mousse with Cherries (page 326): Chill the mousse in shot glasses.

White Chocolate & Blueberry Cheesecake (page 334): Slice into small squares. Serve the blueberry sauce for dipping. Keep in the fridge until ready to serve.

Al dente
The point during cooking at which pasta or vegetables are tender, but retain some bite.

Bake blind
To partially cook a sweet or savory pastry shell before adding the filling, to help keep the pastry crisp in the final dish. The pastry is first lined with parchment and pie weights (baking beans) to prevent air bubbles and shrinkage. The weights and paper are then removed and the pastry is cooked further until dry and pale golden.

Barbecue
A party at which the cooking is done on an outdoor open grill (barbecue), traditionally using charcoal to add a special smoky taste.

Batter
A mixture of flour, beaten egg, and a liquid, such as milk or water, used to make pancakes and to coat food for deep-frying.

Braise
To cook gently in a sealed pan with broth or other liquid, until tender.

Broth (stock)
A flavored cooking liquid obtained by simmering beef, veal, or poultry bones with vegetables and herbs for 2–3 hours. Skim off the fat before use. For speed, a bouillon cube can be dissolved in hot water, and good liquid broths are also available.

Brown
To pan-fry ingredients in very hot fat to color the surface and add flavor.

Casserole dish
A metal, ovenproof glass or ceramic cooking dish with a lid. "Casserole" is also the term for a dish prepared in such a container.

Caramelize
To cook until golden and a little sticky—the point at which the natural sugars in the food start to caramelize.

Char-grill
To cook in a grill pan (griddle) with ridges, or sometimes used in reference to cooking over a grill (barbecue).

Coat
To cover a dish with a substance, such as a sauce.

Cream
To beat butter and sugar together with a whisk or wooden spoon until they become pale and fluffy.

Curdle
Separation of different elements: for example the oil and the egg yolk may curdle when making mayonnaise if the oil is added too quickly. Curdled mixtures will look lumpy and oily.

Deglaze
To pour a liquid, such as wine, broth, or water, into the pan in which meat or vegetables have been fried or roasted to incorporate the sediment on the bottom of the pan into the sauce.

Deseed
To remove the seeds from a fruit or vegetable, first cutting it in half, then scraping out the seeds with a spoon or the tip of a knife.

Drain
To remove the liquid from a food, usually completely, by pouring the food into a colander or strainer and letting all of the liquid pour away. Sometimes you will need to keep the cooking liquid; always check first.

Emulsify
To mix two substances together vigorously to form a blended suspension. Whisking or shaking oil and vinegar together for a salad dressing, or adding butter to egg yolks for hollandaise sauce are good examples.

Floury potatoes
General term used for non-waxy potatoes, such as russet or maris piper. Also known as "maincrop" potatoes. Always bring these up to a boil from cold, rather than adding them to boiling water.

Fluff up
To loosen and separate the grains of rice or couscous once cooked, using the tines of a fork.

Fold
To mix food gently from the bottom of the bowl to the top, in an under-over or figure-of-eight motion that distributes ingredients without knocking out the air.

Glaze
To brush pastry or dough evenly with either milk, egg, or a mixture of both, to give a shiny, golden appearance once baked. Can also apply to meats and vegetables coated in a shiny sauce.

Knead
To work a dough against a work surface with the hands until smooth.

Marinate
To place uncooked meat or other foods in an aromatic or acidic liquid to tenderize it before cooking, or to add extra flavor. Take care not to marinate for too long, as marinades can almost "cook" food, over-tenderizing it and affecting your end result. Marinate delicate fish for no more than a few hours. Meat and chicken can be left in a marinade for up to 24 hours.

Overcrowd a pan

To leave very little space between pieces of food in a pan, whether sautéing, frying, or roasting. This will lead to the food sweating rather than browning or crisping up, giving an inferior result. If in doubt, spread it out.

Part-cover a pan

To leave the lid of a pan slightly askew, so as to let some steam escape. This helps a sauce to reduce, but not overly so.

Pasteurized

Milk, eggs, and cream treated with heat to kill bacteria.

Poach

To cook gently in a liquid such as broth, water, milk, or sugar syrup.

Potato ricer

Rather like a giant garlic press—the potatoes are pressed through fine holes and only need a quick stir to reach a creamy consistency.

Preheat

To set the oven to the desired temperature, and then leave it to become hot. Preheating times can vary drastically from oven to oven, so get to know yours.

Pulse in a food processor

To turn a food processor on and off in short sharp bursts of a second or so (many have pulse buttons for this purpose), to chop ingredients together without blending completely.

Puree

To reduce ingredients to a smooth paste in a food processor or blender. Also the name given to the paste itself.

Raising or rising

The process of increasing the volume of baked goods by adding leavening (raising) agents such as yeast, baking powder, or baking soda (bicarbonate of soda).

Reduce

To boil a liquid to evaporate the water it contains, thereby concentrating the flavor and thickening it.

Resting

Allowing meat to sit out of the oven after roasting and before carving. As meat roasts, the muscle fibers contract, squeezing the juices toward the outer edges. During resting, the fibers relax, letting the juices redistribute within the meat, giving a more succulent result. Meat continues to cook during resting time, so always err on the side of caution with meat timings.

Return to a boil

To let a liquid come back to a full boil once an ingredient has been added to it. Most timings start from this point.

Simmer

To cook slowly over gentle heat. A simmer is the point at which a liquid is about to boil, with just a few bubbles breaking the surface.

Slash

To make a diagonal cut in a piece of fish or meat, and allow flavor into the flesh.

Split

See curdle.

Springform pan

A pan that unclips at the sides to allow easy removal of cakes.

Steep

Refers to leaving something to marinate or for one ingredient to absorb the flavor of another.

Steam

To cook in a perforated container set over boiling water with a tight-fitting lid.

Stuff

To fill the inside of a piece of meat or a vegetable with stuffing.

Sustainably caught fish

Or "eco friendly" fish, from stocks that are not under pressure from over-fishing. Caught by methods that do not negatively impact on the environment.

Syrupy

A term used in reference to sauces, whereby the sauce is thickened down by reduction, to a slightly thicker, and often shiny consistency.

Thicken

To add ingredients, such as flour or egg yolks, to make a sauce or soup thicker.

Well

A hole hollowed out of a mound of flour, into which liquids are added.

Whisk

To beat rapidly with a whisk or electric beaters to increase the volume and aerate ingredients such as egg whites and mayonnaise.

Wilt

To lightly cook leafy vegetables (particularly spinach) until softened, either with hot water or using residual heat from other ingredients.

Zest

The thin outer layer of a citrus fruit, on top of the white pith. Usually finely grated.

Basic Preparations

I've shown you all the necessary instructions for preparing specific vegetables within each recipe, but here's a quick guide to some of the most common ways to slice and chop. A sharp knife is essential, and there's more information about knives on page 14. To hold your chopping board steady, a good tip is to dampen some paper towels and place them under the board.

Coarsely chopped herbs
Pick the leaves from the stems. Rock the knife back and forth a few times over the leaves until they are chopped, but still recognizable.

Finely chopped herbs
Keep chopping until the leaves are fine, but not too fine, as this can impair the flavor and also turn the herbs quite black. Chop the stems as well if the herbs are soft, as they contain a lot of flavor.

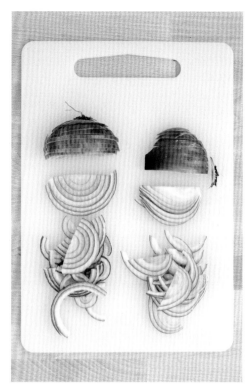

Coarsely chopped onions or shallots

Cut the onion in half through the root. Peel away the skin, then with the flat side of the onion on the board, cut several times through the flesh toward the root, but stopping just before the root itself (you need this to stay attached as it holds the whole thing together). Cut across to release large chunks of onion. For even-sized pieces, I like to make an almost-horizontal cut halfway through the onion before I start slicing.

Finely chopped onions or shallots

The same as for coarsely chopped, but with more slices, made closer together.

Sliced onions or shallots

For pretty petal-shaped slices, halve and peel the onion, trim the root end, then slice from root to tip. Alternatively, just slice the onions into half-moons, then discard the root end.

Thinly sliced garlic

Release the garlic from the bulb, then trim the base of the clove and peel away the skin. Slice thinly.

Crushed garlic

Release the garlic from the bulb, then squash the clove by pushing down on it with the flat side of a large knife. The skin can now be removed easily. Slice, then chop the garlic coarsely. Add a good pinch of salt, then crush the garlic using the edge of a large knife, squashing and scraping it across the board until it becomes a paste.

Shredding vegetables

This is an attractive way to prepare hard vegetables, such as beets (beetroot), carrots, or radishes. You can grate coarsely on a grater if you prefer. Cut in half, then with the flat edge on the board, cut into thin slices. Stack a few slices, then shred into matchsticks and repeat.

Coarsely chopping tomatoes

Halve the tomatoes through the stem, then cut a nick in the top of each piece to remove the hard green core. Cut into wedges, then into chunks.

Sliced tomatoes

Hold the tomato with the stem end facing to the side, not to the top. Some people find a serrated knife best for slicing tomatoes and other soft fruit, and unless your regular knife is properly sharp, then I agree.

Coarsely chopped zucchini (courgettes)

This applies to chopping all long vegetables, whether zucchini, carrots, eggplants (aubergine), or potatoes. First cut into thick slices, stack the slices, cut into sticks, then cut across into large cubes.

Finely chopped zucchini (courgettes)
As for coarsely chopped, but with more slices and sticks made closer together.

Finely chopped chile
Trim the top of the chile, then cut in half along the length. Scrape out the seeds using a teaspoon or the tip of the knife. Thinly slice the flesh along the length, then cut across to make small cubes. Rubber gloves may be worn when handling chiles, which can irritate the skin. Do not touch your eyes during or after handling chiles.

Index

Author's Acknowledgements

It may have my name on the front, but so many people deserve credit for making *Fresh & Easy* what it is. To the team at Phaidon; Emilia Terragni, Laura Gladwin, Michelle Lo and everyone behind the scenes, I really appreciate the care and craft that goes into everything you do. Steven Joyce, thank you for shooting such lovely photographs— I know it wasn't always easy! Rebecca Seal, thanks for being so willing to share your home with us for so long. Huge gratitude to Emily Robertson for the beautiful illustrations too.

The fabulous Katy Greenwood, I can't thank you enough. My co-food stylist, friend and trusted right arm from day one of the shoot, I felt that my recipes were safe in your hands at all stages. Sandra Autukaite, thank you for arranging the ingredients shots so artfully and with such enthusiasm.

Special nods also go to Sue Spaull for recipe testing, and to Linda Doeser and Karen Berman. Speaking of testing, special thanks to everyone who helped with the barbecue chapter—especially Stu and Gem McBride for retesting the ribs, Pip and Matt Edwards for hosting the first meat-fest, and to my Mum, Dad and the Chapman family for the second big cook-out. Also to Anki Noren for the picnic props, my brilliant co-workers at The Old Clinic for their support and healthy appetites, plus Emma Robertson and all of my family and friends. And a huge thank you to Ross, my chief taster, confidant and reason to be cheerful.

Finally, if you are one of the many people who picked up *What to Cook and How to Cook It*, made something from it and wrote to me about it, then thank you too. Your letters were a source of inspiration as I wrote this book – so do let me know what you think.

Jane Hornby

Phaidon Press Inc.
180 Varick Street
New York, NY 10014

Phaidon Press Limited
Regent's Wharf
All Saints Street
London N1 9PA

www.phaidon.com

© 2012 Phaidon Press Limited

ISBN 978 0 7148 6360 3

A CIP catalogue record for this book is available from the British Library.

Commissioning Editor: Laura Gladwin
Project Editor: Michelle Lo
Production Manager: Paul McGuinness

Photographs by Steven Joyce
Illustrations by Emily Robertson
Designed by SML Office

The Publisher would like to thank Julia Hasting, Sophie Hodgkin, Daniel Hurst and Hans Stofregen for their contributions to the book.

Printed in China

NOTE ON THE RECIPES

Some recipes include raw sprouts, uncooked or very lightly cooked eggs, fish or meat. These should be avoided by the elderly, infants, pregnant women, convalescents and anyone with an impaired immune system.